THE
MONEY TALK

Christopher Q. McKay

Dedication

I dedicate this book to my children, Caleb and Shiloh, for whom it is written, and to my wife, Lindsey, without whom it would not be possible.

CONTENTS

INTRODUCTION

I THOUGHT OF WRITING a book for several years but lacked sufficient motivation. I talked to a friend, Mike Holt, and asked him his opinion on my writing a book. Mike then asked me some important questions: "What is your motivation? Is it money, a legacy, or to simply help people?" I admit all three were considerations, but I ultimately determined my children's benefit was the highest priority. They are very young and I am older. What if I wasn't around long enough to teach them all the lessons I have learned about finance? Thinking about my children struggling for decades to reach the same conclusions—if they reached any at all—was an unacceptable outcome, especially if that was partially due to my own laziness in putting my knowledge on paper. I realized it would be worth the effort to write, even if I never sold a single copy.

I have spent years studying finance and investing and I want to pass along all I've learned. My hope is that this book enables my children and others to avoid making the same mistakes I did. I think a great deal of financial blunders occur because people are reluctant to discuss money. This leads to most people not understanding money or investing at all. Growing up, it was considered rude to discuss money and income in my family, and this mindset seems common in our current culture as well. That is truly a shame. We all must use money to live, and to gain real knowledge, it must be discussed. Can you imagine, for instance, if discussing oral hygiene was as taboo as money? You left a toothbrush, toothpaste, and floss in your children's bathroom drawer, but you never actually showed them how to use each tool? They probably wouldn't know what to do and would end up with a mouth full of rotten teeth. Sadly,

The Money Talk

we do this very thing to our children with money, and then we are surprised when they fail. How many people heard the "birds and the bees" speech from their parents? I'll bet at some point, nearly everyone reading remembers this talk. How many of you received the "money" talk? I'm guessing almost nobody. How telling that people feel more compelled to discuss sex with their kids rather than money. That notion would be hysterical if it didn't result in such a hardship for our children. We must talk about sex, but talking about money? Well, that's just too difficult.

My book addresses that very problem. Let's openly, unabashedly, and shamelessly discuss money to educate our children and ourselves. Firstly, let me tell you what I am not: I am not an accountant, and I don't have a PhD in Economics. I'm also not particularly brilliant (but that's good news because that means you are perfectly capable of doing what I've done). I also won't be on the cover of Forbes anytime soon. But here is what I am: a regular guy who decided he did not want to die poor. I am very happy with my financial success. It's not rocket science; my process has worked well, and it is not complicated to replicate. I'm not saying it's not difficult, because it does take time, work, and dedication. However, as Dave Ramsey says, "Personal finance is eighty percent behavior and only twenty percent head knowledge."[1] You might tire of me quoting my idols, but Ramsey is one of my heroes. I also admire Peter Lynch, Warren Buffett, and David Gardner. Isaac Newton once said, "If I have seen further, it is by standing on the shoulders of giants."[2] In the world of money, these men are my giants and you have been forewarned. There are many passages in the Bible that of course reference placing God before money, but there are also many that give insight into how to treat money. Money is not evil. The Bible says, "The love of money is evil,"[3] not money itself. In fact, part of Proverbs 13:22 in the Bible offers this, "A good person leaves an inheritance for their children's children." The following parable from Matthew 25:14-30 gives even more insight.

> *For it is just like a man about to go on a journey, who called his own slaves and entrusted his possessions to them. To one he gave five talents, to another, two, and to another, one, each according to*

his own ability; and he went on his journey. Immediately the one who had received the five talents went and traded with them, and gained five more talents. In the same manner the one who had received the two talents gained two more. But he who received the one talent went away, and dug a hole in the ground and hid his master's money.

Now after a long time the master of those slaves came and settled accounts with them. The one who had received the five talents came up and brought five more talents, saying, "Master, you entrusted five talents to me. See, I have gained five more talents." His master said to him, "Well done, good and faithful slave. You were faithful with a few things, I will put you in charge of many things; enter into the joy of your master." Also the one who had received the two talents came up and said, "Master, you entrusted two talents to me. See, I have gained two more talents." His master said to him, "Well done, good and faithful slave. You were faithful with a few things, I will put you in charge of many things; enter into the joy of your master." And the one also who had received the one talent came up and said, "Master, I knew you to be a hard man, reaping where you did not sow and gathering where you scattered no seed. And I was afraid, and went away and hid your talent in the ground. See, you have what is yours."

But his master answered and said to him, "You wicked, lazy slave, you knew that I reap where I did not sow and gather where I scattered no seed. Then you ought to have put my money in the bank, and on my arrival I would have received my money back with interest." Therefore take away the talent from him, and give it to the one who has the ten talents. For to everyone who has, more shall be given, and he will have an abundance; but from the one who does not have, even what he does have shall be taken away. Throw out the worthless slave into the outer darkness; in that place there will be weeping and gnashing of teeth.

The Money Talk

This gives us perspective on the biblical view of money. It in no way condemns investing money. In fact, I would argue that the Bible advocates thoughtful investing and financial responsibility, being good stewards of what we have been blessed with. Money does not have a conscience. It doesn't care about anyone, and has no moral intent of its own. It is a tool, much like a hammer. A hammer can serve many purposes. It can be used for building a beautiful set of cabinets, smashing priceless artifacts, or even as a weapon. What makes the difference in the outcome? It is solely up to the person who controls it. Much like a hammer, money is a tool that can be used to improve someone's life or destroy it. Managing a large amount of money is a serious responsibility, and it needs to be done carefully and with forethought. George Washington[4] said, "Government is not reason, it is not eloquence — it is force. Like fire, it is a dangerous servant and a fearful master. Never for a moment should it be left to irresponsible action." I would argue that the same thing could be said about money. Left to its own devices, it usually disappears for most of us. We are all forced to deal with money daily and so we may as well learn to do it well.

Much like a hammer, money is a tool that can be used to improve someone's life or destroy it.

There are many people who say money is not important, but as another friend of mine, Avery Scoville[5], so eloquently stated, "Money is like air; it's not important until you don't have it." Money is necessary and important. Like a hammer, it can be used for good or evil; and that is determined by the person in charge of it.

*I've included two bonus chapters: Your To-Do List and Have an Exit Plan. I hope these additional materials help move you closer to your financial goals. When you see a term in bold italic throughout the book, consult the Glossary of Terms for a more detailed explanation.

1

HARD LESSONS

I RELATE SO WELL to Robert Kyosaki and Sharon Lechter's book, *Rich Dad Poor Dad*.[6] Kyosaki's father was a scholar who shunned wealth and money. His friend's father, who was much like Kyosaki's surrogate father, grew up in poverty and had little education, yet he became a self-made millionaire.

My own grandfathers were very much like the men in Kyosaki's book. I spent most of my childhood with them. Both men were born and raised in the South. Both lost their fathers at very early ages and were raised in abject poverty. They both had a strong belief in God. Aside from their faith, family was valued above everything else. They worked very hard and were fiercely independent. My grandfathers were wonderful role models and although I loved them both beyond words, I did not want to emulate either one of them completely.

My maternal grandfather, Papaw Franklin, was a successful building contractor who amassed a lot of wealth. He was an incredible man whom I admired greatly. He took much pleasure in providing for his family and consequently, he was very good at it. Although Papaw Franklin had a fifth-grade education, he worked hard, saved diligently, and built a very profitable business.

After a rather rough childhood, he grew up and married my grandmother.

The Money Talk

They spent their early adult lives working at a bag mill. They saved their wages until Papaw had enough to start a residential contracting business. Papaw Franklin fully embraced hard work and success and therefore operated a profitable business.

Undoubtedly, much of his motivation came from being raised in great poverty. His family didn't even have enough money to buy shoes. Consequently, Papaw had to wear tattered, hand-me-down clothing and shoes. By fifth grade, he was tired of being ridiculed and humiliated by classmates for his tattered attire, and his family needed extra money. So he quit school and began working to help them. As he grew into adulthood in the 1940s, he focused on making money and proving his success to others. However, he never focused on his physical health. He ate poorly, smoked constantly, and lived under substantial stress. He died at the age of fifty-eight, but he was far from ready. I often wish I'd been afforded more time to learn from him.

My paternal grandfather, Papaw Kay, was a very different man, but I loved and respected him just as much as Papaw Franklin. Papaw Kay's father also passed away suddenly when he was young, and he spent much of his childhood in bleak poverty. The peculiar thing is that two men with such similar life circumstances learned vastly different lessons from them.

My Papaw Kay believed that money was evil. He would say things such as, "We are poor, but we are honest." He seemed to believe that wealth was synonymous with dishonesty. Papaw Kay finished high school, and even spent several years in college on a baseball scholarship. However, he quit college during the Great Depression (six credit hours shy of a degree) because he found a job. He held no interest in titles, degrees, or accolades of any sort. He seemed to take it literally from the Bible[7] that, "…it is easier for a camel to go through the eye of a needle than for someone who is rich to enter the kingdom of God." He was a religious man and believed that wealth would diminish his chances of getting into heaven.

He once told me he gave his check to my grandmother and told her, "If you want something and you can pay for it, go ahead." He worked extremely hard to provide for his family and didn't expect the government or anyone else to assist him. He spent most of his life as a carpenter, but was also a skilled farrier and saddle maker. He was well educated and had an extensive vocabulary. He could figure out how to do almost anything. I'm confident he could have been wealthy, but it did not interest him.

On the weekends, Papaw Kay would "hot shoe" horses. For those unfamiliar with the term, "hot shoeing" meant taking his forge to a plantation and shaping shoes to the horse's foot by hammering them into shape while they were red hot. It is back-breaking manual labor; he earned one dollar per foot, and had to supply the shoes. However, his industrious nature paid for their eighty-acre farm.

In his later years he liked "hunting" at deer camp. He really just liked smoking a cigar (Mamaw Kay insisted he give them up), and talking on his C.B. radio while chasing dogs. Like most old men, he still enjoyed hanging out with the guys and sharing a few laughs. Some years later, when it required a three hundred dollar-per-year land lease fee to hunt, he quit going because he couldn't afford it.

I recall a time when I was around twenty-two years old. Papaw Kay needed to go check on the cows. It was raining, and I watched as he slipped plastic bread sacks over his socks at the kitchen table. His boots had holes in them, and the sacks helped to keep his feet dry. Then he pulled on some cheap plastic cowboy boots and went out into the rain. I remember thinking what a shame it was that he had worked so hard his entire life, only to need plastic sacks to keep his feet dry because he couldn't afford new boots. He was getting old by then, and his health was failing. I sure hated to see him struggle. I decided to save enough money to buy him a new pair of Lacrosse rubber boots. Not too long after that, I caught him using the bread sacks again. When I asked him why he wasn't wearing his new boots, he told me he was "saving them." I said, "Look, Papaw, don't save them; wear them. That's why I bought them for you."

I had just turned twenty-eight when Papaw Kay passed away at seventy-eight. While he was much older than my other grandfather, he still did not seem ready to go. He was a man's man and not prone to sentiment.

3

The Money Talk

However, I distinctly remember a conversation we had when he was hospitalized and suffering from congestive heart failure. He explained not long before passing that he didn't know where all the time went. He said to me, "I'm not supposed to be this old."

From both men I learned valuable lessons; some I tried to replicate in my own life, and others I did my best to avoid. Both taught me a strong work ethic and an unshakeable faith in God. I learned to value my family and derived great pleasure from helping them and spending time with them. I also learned that my health was important, and if it failed, I would lose many years with my family. I learned there would be times when my money would be needed to help loved ones. If I didn't have it, I could only offer a limited amount of help. So I made a conscious decision that I did not want to be poor. Don't get me wrong; I didn't find any shame in being broke (because I was). However, I knew I didn't want to live my entire life like that.

I vowed to find my way out of poverty, but admittedly it took some time to figure out. After all, just making the choice didn't allow me to rise to a comfortable place where money was no longer a crushing concern. Other than my Papaw Franklin, who was now gone, I knew few wealthy people and none well enough to question about how to become wealthy. So where would I even begin? I began to study, but not solely from books (although they helped). Instead, I studied behavior. What did successful people do differently to set themselves apart from those who were just mediocre achievers? I noticed that "rich" people often behaved differently than poor people, and I suspected that might be the key. *The Millionaire Next Door* dispelled many of the myths surrounding "millionaires."[8] Here are a few of their findings:

- Millionaires live frugally.
- They buy used cars rather than leasing.
- They live in smaller homes than they can afford, especially while growing their wealth.
- Most of their neighbors are not millionaires.

- Twenty percent of millionaires inherited their wealth. Eighty percent earned it on their own.
- Over half never received an inheritance.
- Nearly half didn't receive financial aid from their families for college.
- Nine out of ten millionaires never received ownership in a family business.
- Self-made millionaires have frugal spouses.
- One area in which millionaires generously spend money is for their children's education.

Rich Habits vs. Poor Habits

Tom Corley also outlined a few of the differences between the habits of the rich and the poor on his website, www.RichHabitsInstitute.com.

- Seventy percent of wealthy people eat less than three hundred junk food calories per day. Ninety-seven percent of poor people eat more than three hundred junk food calories per day.
- Twenty-three percent of wealthy people gamble. Fifty-two percent of poor people gamble.
- Eighty percent of wealthy people are focused on accomplishing some single goal. Only twelve percent of the poor do this.
- Seventy-six percent of wealthy people exercise aerobically four days a week. Twenty-three percent of poor people do this.
- Sixty-three percent of wealthy people listen to audio books during commute to work versus five percent of poor people.
- Eighty-one percent of wealthy people maintain a to-do list versus nineteen percent of poor people.
- Sixty-three percent of wealthy parents make their children read two or more nonfiction books a month versus three percent of poor people.

- Seventy percent of wealthy parents make their children volunteer ten hours or more a month versus three percent of poor people.
- Eighty percent of wealthy make 'Happy Birthday' calls versus eleven percent of poor people.
- Sixty-seven percent of wealthy people write down their goals versus seventeen percent of poor people.
- Eighty-eight percent of wealthy people read thirty minutes or more each day for education or career reasons versus two percent of poor people.
- Six percent of wealthy people say what's on their mind versus sixty-nine percent of poor people.
- Seventy-nine percent of wealthy people network five hours or more each month versus sixteen percent of poor people.
- Sixty-seven percent of wealthy people watch one hour or less of TV daily versus twenty-three percent of poor people.
- Six percent of wealthy people watch reality TV versus seventy-eight percent of poor people.
- Forty-four percent of wealthy people wake up three hours before work starts versus three percent of poor people.
- Seventy-four percent of wealthy teach good daily success habits to their children versus one percent of poor people.
- Eighty-four percent of wealthy people believe good habits create opportunity luck versus four percent of poor people.
- Seventy-six percent of wealthy believe bad habits create detrimental luck versus nine percent of poor people.
- Eighty-six percent of wealthy believe in lifelong educational self-improvement versus five percent of poor people.
- Eighty-six percent of wealthy people love to read versus twenty-six percent of poor people.

Rich or Poor is Behavioral

The Brookings Institution is a century-old American research group in

Washington, D.C. that conducts research and education in the social sciences- primarily in economics, metropolitan policy, governance, foreign policy, and global economy and development. The Brookings Institute has extensively studied the behaviors of both rich and poor people, and they have whittled the analysis down to three simple rules. You can avoid poverty by:

1. **Graduating from high school.**
2. **Waiting to get married until after age twenty-one and not having children until after marriage.**
3. **Having a full-time job.**

The Brookings Institute says by doing these three things, the chance of falling into poverty is just two percent. You'll also have a seventy-four percent chance of being in the middle class. I'm sure we can all name someone who is successful despite violating one of those rules. However, if your chances of success are practically guaranteed by following those three simple rules, why tempt fate?

My focus here is to show that avoiding poverty is primarily behavioral. We all fall into habits (good and bad) after we become accustomed to certain things. These habits become behavior patterns and these behaviors affect our ability to build wealth.

As if you needed further proof that rich versus poor is behavioral, I offer you this via Dr. Thomas Sowell, an American economist, social theorist, political philosopher, and author. He is currently Senior Fellow at the Hoover Institution at Stanford University. Sowell was born in North Carolina, but grew up in Harlem, New York. He dropped out of high school and served in the United States Marine Corps during the Korean War. He received a bachelor's degree, graduating magna cum laude from Harvard University in 1958 and a master's degree from Columbia University in 1959. In 1968, he earned his Doctorate in Economics from the University of Chicago.

In his book *Wealth, Poverty, and Politics*, Dr. Sowell states that politicians often describe middle-class people as "rich" simply to tax them.[9] Notwithstanding, most people do not stay within the same economic strata their entire lives. Some wealthy people later become poor; others who are poor later amass wealth. There are also many who are transitioning between the two. When you talk about rich and poor people, you are often talking about the same segment of the population. However, your behavior dictates where you move on the rich/poor spectrum and how long you stay there.

There is so much chatter about "income inequality" and "how unfair the system is." I find this amusing because often these are the same people. As I have stated before, I'm not rich but I'm in the upper strata on the economic scale and have been very near the bottom strata by U.S. standards. Why the movement? Behavior. When you do stupid stuff like spend your last five dollars to sneak alcohol into a bar, and hours later, have no money to buy food and I'll explain more about this later.

This is not the behavior of someone making sound financial decisions. My five-dollar decision had a predictable outcome, yet I did it anyway. I paid for that stupidity and learned from it. According to Dr. Sowell, very few people remain permanently in the very upper or lower economic strata. It's also fairly predictable that when someone enters the job market with little skill, their standard of living will improve as they age. If they don't know how to invest though, that level will decline when the income disappears. Some people don't like to think about old age and others don't know how to invest, even if they do understand what will happen this often leads to extreme hardship.

Do you need even further proof that your behavior determines your financial outlook? Enter best-selling lottery and structured settlement expert, Don McNay, who points out that within two years of retirement, seventy-eight percent of NFL football players are bankrupt or under financial stress.[10] Sixty percent of NBA basketball players are broke within five years of retirement.

Mike Tyson reportedly bought three tigers for $140,000 and had to spend $12,000 per month for their care. He shelled out $144,000 each year to keep them. Shortly after that, he declared bankruptcy. Who would have seen that coming?

It's simple; if you want to be well off, model the behavior of wealthy people. How do the wealthy behave? Stanley's *The Millionaire Next Door* addresses that question. You will undoubtedly hear people refer to the "invisible rich." These are people who live well within their means; they are inconspicuous about their consumption, and many people are clueless about their wealth. They don't buy flashy cars or spend thousands embellishing their teeth with diamonds. They don't buy tigers either. They are regular people who build wealth slowly.

According to Stanley's research, the invisible rich are middle-aged men who have been married to the same woman for many years. They have two to three kids and usually own a dog. They have lived in the same neighborhood for years, and their neighbors have no idea how wealthy they are. Dr. Stanley refers to this group of people as **PAW: Prodigious Accumulators of Wealth**. Consequently, he refers to people who spend more than they earn as **UAW: Under Accumulators of Wealth**.

What separates one from the other? Behavior, of course. Many UAW are actually very high wage earners. Note that they still may have a very low net worth, despite all the shiny possessions that seem to indicate wealth. Dr. Stanley refers to this as "Big hat, no cattle." Which would you rather have? I'd prefer the cattle.

Living Within Your Means

Why do I bring this up? The main reason is to point out the importance of "living within your means." What exactly does that mean anyway? While there are many euphemisms for the phrase, generally it means spending less money than you earn. Ramsey suggests you "…live like no one else, so that later you can live like no one else." The poor may call that concept "being tight" or *codo* in Spanish. You probably know even more derogatory phrases to describe this behavior. They all have one theme in common: they describe a person who spends less than or equal to his earnings.

In this world of instant credit and instant gratification, living within your means is often rejected as old-fashioned thinking. However, being successful with money requires you to not only live within your means, but often *below* them. Living beneath your means is spending less than your total wages.

If you merely live *within* your means and spend exactly what you earn, you have nothing leftover to save or invest. If an extra hundred dollars in your checking account gives you the urge to spend it frivolously, you are just living within your means. You must release limiting behaviors such as this to experience financial victory. If you want to have money to invest in the first place, you need to live beneath your means. This again leads back to behavior.

If you live like a rich person before you are actually rich, you will probably never become rich. If you spend money carefully, saving and investing, you will be successful in accumulating wealth. If you flagrantly spend money trying to impress others, you probably will never be wealthy. Decide to have the cattle and not the big hat. After all, do you really care what other people think if you are able to retire comfortably? Is it important what other people think if you have the security of no debt, a paid-for home, cars and your children's education paid for? If being affluent is more important than appearing affluent, "Act like it," as my father always says.

Are appearances more important to you than the truth? I ask because that is essentially the choice you will have to make. Ramsey's radio show introduction, in part, states, "...the paid-off home mortgage has taken the place of the BMW as the status symbol of choice."[11] You may not have a lot of bling and people won't openly know your house is paid off, but I prefer that alternative over having a nice vehicle in the driveway. I'm not too concerned about what people think; I'm after the cattle, not the big hat.

If being affluent is more important than appearing affluent, act like it.

I hope I have convinced you that financial success is behavioral and that you need to live beneath your means. Let's look at one easy way to do that. Transportation. Do you know anyone who equates success with driving a new car? I have known countless people who replace their vehicles every two years. In fact, many of those folks also keep a car note for their entire lives. It is a cycle of paying one car off, trading it in immediately for a new one, and paying another note. Here's a little secret: if you can't pay cash for the vehicle, you can't afford it. Many people don't realize that paying cash for and driving used reliable vehicles can make the difference between retiring comfortably or not being able to retire.

If you maintain a constant car note from age twenty-five until age sixty-five, it will cost you dearly. If you instead invested $400 per month in an index mutual fund, at the end of forty years you would have $2,336,933.86. Again, if you listen to Ramsey's radio show, you will hear him ask his caller about the car note; then, he typically tells the caller to sell the car. This is one of the best ways to live beneath your means. You don't have to drive a clunker all your life, but if you can't save for retirement, then you can't afford a car payment. As your wealth grows, you can afford nicer things. Keep in mind that your wealth will grow as time passes, and the amount of income will grow also. That means that "living beneath your means" will generally lead to a better standard of living than you currently enjoy. Some people can't seem to wrap their head around that and instead say, "Well, I just can't live like that."

What they fail to remember is that living in a small house or driving a used car is just temporary. Starting the process can be rather unpleasant. Living in a tiny apartment while you climb out of debt, but later paying cash for a $30,000 vehicle while you still spend beneath your means—that is worth the sacrifice. Owning a quarter-million-dollar home or a small ranch free and clear sure makes up for a lot sack lunches.

Some believe there is no causation; being rich is simply luck. Still others suggest it is the government's duty to provide us with a cozy lifestyle. I disagree with those notions entirely. Being wealthy is behavioral; it's choosing a lifestyle that facilitates it and then living that lifestyle. I didn't discover Stanley and Ramsey until I was far along in my financial journey, but they are certainly both worth reading. We have limitless access to knowledge now, so take advantage of it. I talk to quite a few people about finance and I enjoy it immensely. I have been extremely broke, and I have been financially secure. It truly isn't all about the money; it's all the things money affords you. Having experienced both poverty and abundance, I much prefer not having to worry about money.

While I may not be considered rich by *Forbes* standards, my wife Lindsey and I amassed several hundred acres of land and a home, all while still in my forties. We own our vehicles, and hold a substantial amount of investments in the stock market while still managing to save for our children's college education. While we have no debt and don't owe a nickel to anyone, we also don't lead an extravagant lifestyle. But it is a comfortable one. In a few short years, I will be eligible to retire, and I can't wait to spend even more time with my family. More important than retirement eligibility though, is that I will be financially *able* to retire. I say *able* because I don't mean quitting and seeing how things go. I mean having a plan in place.

For us, that means everything will be paid off and we will have a steady, predictable retirement income. That sounds great, but you may be asking just *how* that is possible. After all, I certainly didn't get an inheritance, I haven't won the lottery or a lawsuit, nor has the government's generosity led to my prosperity. It was all due to hard work, sacrifice, and learning how to save and invest. Most people hit sixty-five years old and just decide to retire and see what happens. Hitting a certain age does not magically make you able to retire. Being able means having the financial means to pursue your own interests with dignity, no matter the age.

Hitting a certain age does not magically make you able to retire.

Bottom Line: Building wealth is not about "luck." It involves behavior, hard work, and setting goals—and continuing that behavior until you reach them, or perhaps forever.

2

CONVENTIONAL WISDOM= FAULTY ASSUMPTIONS

Do you believe that luck determines wealth? If so, you might be falling into the **conventional wisdom** trap. *Conventional wisdom* is defined as *the generally accepted belief, opinion, judgment, or prediction about a particular matter.*[12] Now that you understand what conventional wisdom is, let's take it a step further and find out what it is in relation to money. What are some generally accepted truths about money? One is that we all need it—which is accurate. Another is that it's considered impolite (and maybe a little embarrassing) to discuss. Conventional wisdom says that if we get a good job and work hard, it will all be okay.

Perhaps you've heard that if you're poor, you will always be poor, so why try to dig your way out? Does this sound familiar? For those of us with any plan at all, it probably looks something like this: "I'll get a good education, find a stable, well-paying job, and live off the extra." How do I define *extra*? Well, it's the difference between what you make and what is required for you to pay your bills; your fluff money. Look at your personal finances for just a minute. How's that *fluff* treating you right now? Is it making all your dreams come true? I'm guessing you wouldn't need to read this book if your fluff money was adequate to accomplish your dreams. So why do we consistently buy into conventional wisdom? Perhaps that's because it is comfortable; these are ideas some of us have heard all our lives.

Let's first look at the people who have given up. This is often referred to as "learned helplessness," a concept discovered accidentally by psychologists Martin Seligman and Steven F. Maier.[13] They initially observed helpless behavior in dogs that were conditioned to expect an electrical shock after hearing a tone. One group of dogs could exhibit a particular behavior and escape the stimulus, but the other group could not escape, no matter what happened. After receiving the adverse stimulus for a while, the dogs stopped trying to escape the stimulus; they wouldn't even try to escape the shock even if it could be easily avoided. They had learned helplessness.

Humans exhibit the very same behavior. They frequently invent all kinds of excuses as to why they can't be successful. In a Reader's Digest article from September 1947, Henry Ford said, "Whether you believe you can do a thing or not, you're right."[14] I tend to agree with Mr. Ford.

You will notice that many of my favorite authors and heroes are not conventional. Ramsey and Lynch, Warren Buffett, the Gardner brothers from Motley Fool—they are unconventional. Why do I like them so much? The reason is simple—conventional wisdom is often wrong. Many people have incorrect preconceived notions about money. Many automatically make decisions without questioning them. Then they carry them out habitually, with no thought given to how bad the results are, or if they could do any better.

Society is programmed to believe debt is a normal, unavoidable part of life. People buy houses they can't afford on a thirty-year mortgage. They buy luxury cars, Harley Davidson motorcycles, and extra "toys" on credit. Before we go any further, I'm not advocating that you go your entire life without borrowing money. You will probably need to at some point, and that's all right. For example, if you have no other way to afford college, you may have to borrow money. But that is different from renting a nice apartment while you're attending college because you don't like the less expensive dorms. Simply put, you can absolutely bypass purchasing a lavish nicety on credit. Like I mentioned earlier, why purchase a new car when a used one will do? That type of debt is completely avoidable.

However, these excessive spending habits are now routine; people do this routinely without any question as to whether it is best for them. This kind of logic seems to say, "What is the sense in fighting conventional wisdom? You can just borrow money to buy whatever you want and it becomes affordable because you're making payments."

Conventional wisdom also tells us lies such as: the stock market is the equivalent of shooting craps, and that if we are poor, we will always be poor. Did you know that somewhere north of eighty percent of all millionaires are first generation?[15] This fact alone pokes a few holes in the conventional wisdom myth about always being poor, doesn't it?

That's why we should at times, challenge conventional wisdom. We should stand back and really scrutinize things accepted as truth. The most dangerous part of conventional wisdom as it relates to money is that people handle it so badly. It never ceases to amaze me that those who are so broke they can't pay attention are those constantly judging people who are doing very well financially.

I read about a study involving four caged monkeys.[16] In the center of the cage was a tall pole with a bunch of bananas suspended from the ceiling. One of the four monkeys climbed up the pole and tried to grab the bananas. Just as he did this, he was hit with a torrent of cold water from a fire hose. He scurried back down the pole without the bananas. Eventually, the other three tried it with the same results. Finally, they realized that when one climbed the pole, they would all get sprayed. Then, they removed one of the four monkeys and replaced him with a new one. The new monkey entered the room, saw the bananas and decided to go for it. Just as he was about to scamper up the pole, the other three pulled him back down. After a while, he learned the message that something bad would happen if any of the monkeys attempted to reach those bananas. Researchers continued replacing an existing monkey with a new one. Each time a new monkey would try to climb the pole, and the others would pull him down. Eventually, all the original monkeys who had been sprayed were replaced with monkeys who had never been sprayed. Although none of them understood *why* they shouldn't climb the pole, they knew to stay away from it. These monkeys not only learned to be helpless, they learned to keep anyone else from being successful also.

This reminds me very much of the stock market. The Great Depression began in 1929, and the stock market plummeted. There are very few people living today who were alive at that time, much less affected by it. Yet it left such an indelible impression that many still fear the stock market because of it.

The cause of the stock market collapse is often taken out of context. Many of the losses surrounding the collapse were caused by people who used leverage to buy stocks on the margin. I won't go into too much detail about how this works, but buying stocks on margin means purchasing stocks with borrowed money. If your stock drops and there is a *margin call*, the stock broker sells them at a loss and you are on the hook for the rest. At that time, it was something like ten percent down, so with $10, you could buy $100 worth of stock. When the stock declined, they could sell your $10 worth of stock at a loss and you had to come up with the other $90. In many cases, people had leveraged their entire life savings to buy on margin, and it was sold at a fraction of its worth when the market dropped. As a result, they were broke, had lost their life savings, and owed many times more money than the value of their life savings.

Don't borrow money to buy stocks. If you stick to buying stocks with money that is yours, the most you can lose is your initial **investment.** Your loss can't go any higher than that. You can only lose your original investment if you follow this advice. There is no upside limit; you can make money for many, many years and there is no limit on how much you can make. Your investment can double or grow ten, one hundred, or one-thousand-fold, depending on how good the company is. In short, you have a limited downside and an unlimited upside. The key is this: do not borrow money to buy stocks.

Many of those fearful of investing may not understand the difference between short-term and long-term investments. Had the Great Depression era investors bought solid companies before the market collapse and held them long-term, they would have recuperated their investment and then some. In fact, if they had invested just $10,000 in the strongest twenty companies one day before the market collapsed, they would have eventually wound up rich without adding any additional money. While it would have taken several years to get back to even, the point here is that they would have. From there, it would have grown. Had they continued to add money every month regardless, their wealth would have increased even more rapidly. The chart below illustrates this point. If you ignore short-term fluctuations and invest for long-term benefit, you will inevitably come out ahead. Whenever people who know nothing about the market whatsoever start telling you that you are going to lose it all, they are the equivalent of the monkeys who have never been sprayed pulling you off the ladder. Take my advice: ignore the other monkeys. For many of us, the stock market is the greatest wealth-building tool we have at our disposal.

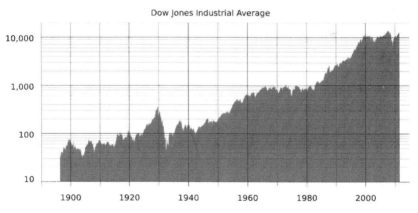

Dow Jones Industrial Average, courtesy of Wikipedia

Why is the stock market such a strong wealth-building tool? This is due to the tremendous growth of the American economy and thus businesses over the last 150 years or so.

The Money Talk

For many of us, the stock market is the greatest wealth-building tool we have at our disposal.

This tremendous growth is not difficult to understand. An entire family with a mule used to farm forty acres just to feed themselves and scratch out a living. Now, one farmer with a couple of farm hands and good tractors can farm a few hundred acres, producing more than many, many families once could. This frees up all those other men and family members to produce things. Consequently, productivity has exploded. One man running a track hoe can move more earth than scores of miners once could, freeing up all those miners to do other jobs. Good old capitalism lets men pursue their own interests and produce all this wealth. The stock market is a vehicle that lets you reap the benefits from this explosion in production.

Compared to those living during our nation's early history, we enjoy an amazing standard of living in America. We have better entertainment, healthcare, food choices, and living conditions than kings used to enjoy. Most of us can drive down the street to a fast-food place of our choice and in minutes, get more food than we can eat for a mere $10. In many countries all over the world, people spend nearly every cent they earn to merely buy food, often doing back-breaking manual labor to earn it. In the U.S., most people spend a small fraction of their paycheck on food.

There will always be exceptions, but poor people can afford to be fat for the first time in the history of the world right here in the United States. People get on their iPads, smart phones, and home computers to complain about income inequality. They complain about the "capitalists" taking advantage of them and stealing from them, not paying "their fair share."

In the meantime, most people the world over have a higher standard of living than ever before. And arguably as Americans, we enjoy the highest standard of living compared to anywhere else in the world. Other countries frequently envy the U.S. due to our bigger houses, nicer cars, and better food choices.

I'm not saying we don't have our problems, but I'm glad I live during this time in this country. We are wealthier and freer than almost anywhere at any time in history. Do you know why? The American economy and much-maligned capitalism have made this possible. Bash the United States all you want, but there will always be Americans creating wealth without having to be regulated, managed, or directed. What we require most is limited interference from the government where it can possibly be avoided. With that said, if you want to increase your wealth and change your family tree, hitch your wagon to the greatest wealth-building machine ever seen, the American economy. What is one of the best ways to do that? Own stocks; own a share of a wonderful company managed by a great manager. It's an amazing tool for creating a fortune for yourself and your family.

However, the "monkeys" will tell you to avoid this *dangerous* wealth-building tool. Or, you may get the flipside: cliché advice such as, "The stock market is easy; just buy low and sell high." That is very simple counsel, but much easier said than done. I've never actually met anyone who gave this advice and followed it. That type of logic reminds me of my son, Caleb, when he offers to cook pancakes. He has good intentions, but he doesn't realize that he must measure batter, add key ingredients, and turn on the stove. He doesn't know the pancakes should be flipped at the proper time, nor does he know when the pancakes are finished. He simply doesn't know what he doesn't know.

This is often referred to as the Dunning–Kruger Effect, a cognitive bias wherein relatively unskilled individuals suffer from illusory superiority, mistakenly assessing their ability to be much higher than is accurate.[17] It was first experimentally observed by David Dunning and Justin Kruger (Cornell University) in 1999.

This is the category in which many financial writers fall. They believe average working people know far more than they do about the stock market. So, when people tell you "buy low and sell high," and since they have absolutely no clue as to what "high" and "low" are, you would probably conclude that this is an impossible task for them. Me too.

If you hear Warren Buffett or Peter Lynch say that a stock is "expensive," they are using metrics like price to earnings (P/E) or other similar measure to draw that conclusion. Generally, those who encourage you to buy low and sell high have no idea what a P/E is.

Of course, these folks are on the opposite end of the spectrum when compared to those who have given up. They imagine that they can just jump in and buy and sell stocks like crazy without doing any real work and still get rich. The Dunning-Krueger Effect also states that people who are very competent at a given task overestimate the abilities of others because it is so easy for them. This is the category in which many financial writers fall. They believe average working people know far more than they do about the stock market.

Most us fall somewhere on the spectrum. There are those who know nothing and are scared to death of the market—that's most people. Then there are those who know nothing and are unaware of it; they don't know enough to be fearful—those are a few people. Then we have the people who understand things easily and know quite a lot; they assume everyone else does too. The first two groups are those you will usually encounter. They are quite willing to give advice, regardless of their subject knowledge or financial situation.

I want you to migrate toward the informed end of the spectrum while realizing your limitations. Realize that you do not have to be a stockbroker to make money with stocks. I'm not an investing guru, but I make good money from investments.

Still, there are others who are fearful they will "waste" their money by not spending all of it before they die. These people want to live for today, and not consider tomorrow. That is their right, but let's look at that logic from a farming perspective. Before farmers could buy seeds commercially, they had to save enough corn kernels each year for replant the following spring. If they had a good crop, that task was easy. In lean years when they had a poor crop yield and barely enough food to eat, they may have been tempted to eat the last dozen ears, thus enjoying a good meal.

However, the farmer would remember that each corn kernel could potentially become a new stalk and produce several hundred kernels of corn.

It was possible, even probable, that some of those planted kernels would be picked up by birds or eaten by worms, and still others might rot in the ground. But every year that he didn't save his seed corn meant starvation the following year. There would be hardship during the lean years, but the absence of seed corn would certainly end in tragedy. This example is very much like investing; each dollar you save has the potential to become hundreds given enough time. The spenders out there may call you foolish, but do you really benefit from their advice?

It's like listening to a four-hundred-pound man with a 210/100 blood pressure reading give you pointers on improving your cardio. If he could barely walk from his car to a restaurant without stopping to rest, would you take his advice very seriously? Probably not. If you were the overweight man, would you feel compelled to give advice to a fitness enthusiast in the first place? Probably not.

People who are completely broke (the overweight gentleman) feel perfectly comfortable counseling those (the jogger) who are financially stable. Advice like "You know what you should buy? Another house!" and "If I had your money, I would go buy…" Generally, those same broke people also hurl insults. My favorite is, "He is so tight that he squeaks." when referring to someone with financial security. In broke-people speak, that translates into, "He lives within his means" or "He doesn't buy things he can't afford." I find this especially amusing when the broke people who claim to be generous find out that the "miser" gives far more of his money away as a percentage of income than they do. I guess things are not always as they seem.

All kidding aside, I have nothing against those who are overweight or broke. But I *am* calling out people who think they should share their opinion in an area in which they have utterly failed, or who judge financially responsible people when they themselves are reckless in that department. I'm unapologetic that way.

<u>What is Normal?</u>

If you pick up any of Ramsey's books (and I hope you do), you will discover that "normal" is broke. Normal (conventional) is living paycheck to paycheck. Normal is struggling constantly all your life to pay for stuff you don't need. "We buy things we don't need with money we don't have to impress people we don't like."[18]

Therefore I don't put much stock in conventional wisdom. It tells you not to pay off your mortgage early, or you'll lose that sweet end-of-year tax deduction (that is wrong, and I'll explain why later). It tells you that investing in the stock market is too risky when it is probably the greatest chance many of us will ever have to retire comfortably (more on that later too). Are you now beginning to see that wisdom and conventional wisdom are not the same things at all?

Often there is nothing wise about conventional wisdom.

Did you know the average American retiree sixty-five and over has saved only $56,000 towards retirement? And workers under thirty-five barely have $6,000 in savings?[19] Almost one third of workers (twenty-eight percent) say they have less than $1,000 in savings and investments that could be used for retirement, not counting their primary residence or defined benefits.[20] Ouch.

Clearly, these are people who just cross their fingers and hope for the best. In case you were wondering, this isn't Kansas, and you aren't Dorothy. You can't click your heels together and say, "There's no place like home." and everything magically gets better. I guess you could always buy some red shoes and a gingham dress, but I'm pretty sure that won't help your situation. [21] In all seriousness, these are alarming statistics. Undoubtedly, there will be plenty of suffering and hardship ahead for many of those included in the data. Yet that is generally the road down which conventional wisdom leads.

<u>Faulty Assumptions</u>

Throughout my life, I have known people who were convinced they would receive an inheritance. Their parents were neither rich nor poor, but the kids just knew Mom and Dad were going to leave them a nice house, a farm, money, or something else of value. This perceived "windfall" later helped them justify why they were simply treading water and enjoying themselves in the present and not preparing for the future. I'm not condemning anyone who receives an inheritance. It's just that this type of plan rarely works out. I suppose it's wonderful to inherit something (I wouldn't know), but all too often, people use the promise of an inheritance as a primary plan when it should just be a fallback plan.

I liken it to camping without a tent and hoping it doesn't rain. However, retiring broke is a lot worse than spending one night wet and miserable. Worse yet, it tears families apart. People become resentful and desperate when they don't receive the money they had ear-marked for their "retirement plan." They become angry and bitter when it must be used for a parent's long-term care or frequent hospital stays.

> ### *People use the promise of an inheritance as a primary plan when it should just be a fallback plan.*

Even when an inheritance is received, it's often a source of contention that leads to siblings despising one another over perceived wrongdoing. Still I have seen others who "lost" their inheritance because the surviving parent used that money to feed an addiction problem. What is the easiest way to avoid this kind of mess from ruining your life? Plan on not getting anything. Plan instead to earn it yourself. Then if you do happen to inherit something, you will be pleasantly surprised.

The scenarios above all have a common thread: relying on conventional wisdom and faulty assumptions will lead to disappointment. I'm glad that by the time I was in college, I knew that I would never inherit anything. My dad always said that upon his death, if his wife wrote a check to the undertaker and it bounced, he had it figured out just right. I am thankful for his honesty. I never planned on receiving an inheritance, and I always knew that if I wanted anything, I would have to make it myself.

While my parents are both still living, I know that receiving an inheritance isn't a possibility. If you are fortunate enough to receive an inheritance, that's great. But certainly don't count on it.

Bottom Line: Sometimes you need to challenge conventional wisdom; especially when it's telling you that you should just settle for "broke." Don't rely on others to leave you wealthy or fund your retirement. Be honest about your reality.

3

HARD TIMES

WHEN I GRADUATED FROM high school in 1985, the construction industry in north Louisiana was in the toilet. That was bad news for me. I had spent a lot of time working construction jobs with my dad (a very skilled carpenter and builder), as well as my papaws (Papaw Kay was a carpenter and cabinet maker; Papaw Franklin was a contractor, remember?). Consequently, I was skilled at carpentry. By the time I turned eighteen, I knew how to lay out and frame houses, and set concrete forms. Would you believe I still have that original W-2 tax form from 1985? Want to guess how much I made? The year I graduated from high school, I earned a whopping $1,882.75. I did any kind of work I could find (and I mean anything), and that's where I finished at year's end. Yes, I know there has been some *inflation* since then, and I graduated in May, so only seven full months were spent trying to find work. But even with those obvious variables considered, it is still a pitiful amount.

Do you know where I keep that original W-2? You'll find it taped over my office desk, and with good reason. It reminds me of where I started. I made a lot of mistakes and will no doubt make many more. But I've also done a lot of things right; I hope you can learn from both. I know people tire of the "I had it so hard when I was a kid." and "I walked five miles to school everyday uphill both ways in the snow." stories. But for having grown up in the United States, I legitimately had some pretty tough times. My brother and I both lived with my dad for a while shortly after high school graduation. Since we were all in the construction trade, times were lean for us. I never went "hungry," but I *did* choke down a lot of food that I didn't care for because I couldn't afford anything else.

I remember grocery shopping with my dad and brother. We would figure out who was going to eat what. If we all ate it, we split the bill for those items three ways. If it was an item only I ate (like Cotto salami), I had to pay for it myself. Since we couldn't afford much at the grocery, and enjoyed hunting, we were lucky to have collected a pile of rabbits from the year before. That year, we ate boiled rabbits, baked rabbits, fried rabbits, rabbit gumbo... I think you get the picture. For years afterward, just the smell of a rabbit cooking would turn my stomach, and I have a very strong stomach (unless my children get sick; just ask my wife).

On one occasion, I found a handful of overlooked shotgun shells. I took my find down to Bayou Bartholomew and shot a couple wood ducks behind Papaw Kay's farm. When I came in that evening, my brother was cooking. I told him that we had been eating rabbits for so long, that even ducks cooking smelled like rabbits now. He replied, "I was saving the ducks for a special occasion." When I indignantly informed him that it was a special occasion because we had something to eat besides rabbits, a fistfight nearly ensued. But by ages eighteen and nineteen, we had gone knuckle and skull enough times to decide it wasn't worth it.

During this time I slept on an old hand-me-down mattress on the floor of my dad's house. There was no box spring and no bed frame; I literally just had a mattress lying on the bedroom floor. I was absolutely mortified when my brother brought a couple of girls over, and they saw where I slept. Papaw Kay, God bless him, found out and took some old angle iron he found at Moeller's Motorcycle shop and welded a bed frame for me. Like I mentioned before, he was resourceful and could make something out of anything.

Hard Times

These were some of the leanest times I had experienced. I worked for a couple of years as a carpenter, and while things improved slightly due to the construction industry's recovery, life was still pretty rough. If it rained, we often were not able to work. That meant using all my savings to stay afloat until the weather dried out again. There was no sick leave, no annual leave, no *401(k)*, and no insurance of any sort. If I needed something, I had to figure out where it would come from. It seemed like every time I spent a couple months saving a few extra hundred dollars, we would run out of work or the weather would not cooperate. Then, it would wipe out my savings completely and I'd be back to square one. I soon discovered I was not the only one struggling like this. Every year, the whole crew would plan on taking time off for the first week of deer season. And every year, it would rain for a few days and wipe out everyone's savings and they couldn't afford to go.

I found something else out much earlier in my career about saving and getting ahead. Every time I received a raise (usually $1 per hour), that money would be absorbed quickly. I couldn't figure out where it went or how I had survived before on less money.

It was a pitifully small amount, but jumping from $4 to $5 per hour felt like I was rolling in the dough. So I would buy a couple things with the extra money, and then I would start saving the extra $40 per week and finally get ahead. By the time I had bought a couple of things I "really wanted" I had become accustomed to living off the extra money and didn't know how I had made it before on less money.

Each time I got a raise it was the same story. It took many years and several jobs before I realized that a much better answer was to save or invest that extra raise money.

After you become accustomed to putting the money into a savings or investing account, you never miss it. The next time you receive a financial windfall (i.e. pay raise, tax return, or inheritance check), remember this: If you immediately start saving that extra money, you will never miss it because you weren't used to having it in the first place. However, if you do the reverse (spend first, attempt to save later), you will struggle. Take my word for it.

Bottom Line: Don't be afraid of change. If you don't change your life, no one else will do it for you. Transform your behaviors and you transform your life.

4

HARD TIMES CONTINUE

ONE FATEFUL NIGHT AROUND Christmas 1986, I was drinking with my brother and three buddies at my dad's house. The carpentry gig was not working out so well, and while I knew I could survive, I also saw that the rest of my life would be spent struggling from one paycheck to the next. That night, knowing that military service would give us a shot at free college education, we made a pact to sign up with the Army National Guard recruiter the following Monday. The next morning, however, once the alcohol had left their systems, nearly everyone had changed their mind. My buddy Brent and I were the only ones who followed through and joined the Louisiana Army National Guard. My brother, Brian, was able to discover other avenues to pay for college, so it all worked out.

Years after graduating college, I told Mamaw Franklin the above story. She had always said nothing good could ever come from alcohol, and I told her jokingly that in my case, she was wrong, and owed me an apology. She never quite saw it my way, so we just agreed to disagree. I don't drink much alcohol, but I always enjoyed a good laugh at my Mamaw's expense.

While I had finally decided that college was the answer, no one in my family could afford to help me. So, first things first. I spent five months at Basic Training and AIT (Advanced Individual Training) in Fort Leonard

The Money Talk

Wood, Missouri. For the first one and a half years, I attended college at Louisiana Tech. I had no car, so Mamaw Franklin would pick me up on the weekends and loan me her car. I was twenty years old, almost twenty-one, when I started college, and still had to borrow my grandmother's car on the weekend. She would give me $20 she could scarcely afford, or buy me a can of Skoal on the weekend. It was the best thing ever.

The National Guard paid for college, so between drill weekends and the G.I. bill, I received a whopping $240 every month during the school year (about $8 dollars per day) whether I needed it or not. I still had to buy my own books and clothes, as well as pay for any other expenses that popped up. This was barely enough money to scrape by on; I remember going out to *Muthers* on a couple of weekends. *Muthers* was a local dance club and I only went a few times because I simply couldn't afford it. I would go out with $5 in my pocket. I would spend $2 on a bottle of Canadian Hunter, pay the $1 cover charge, and pay $1 for a Coke (for mixing with the Canadian Hunter). The remaining $1 was spent tipping the bartender. At the end of the night, when everyone else wanted to hit Taco Bell, I would just tell them I was full. I didn't have any money left over for tacos. It does beg the question: Why on Earth was I spending my last $5 partying instead of just buying the tacos, right? I have no logical answer, other than blaming it on stupidity.

I finally transferred to Northeast Louisiana University so I could be closer to home and work part-time. I did this with the purpose of buying my own vehicle. I soon bought a well-used Toyota truck from my brother for $2,200. I spent several days a week, along with weekends, doing construction work to pay for it. It was a lot of money and quite a commitment, but I took over the notes because I was tired of not having transportation. I would go to class all day Monday. On Tuesdays and Thursdays, I would work all day and then rush to night class for three hours. I worked until noon every Wednesday, and then I would hurry to my afternoon class. Every Friday was spent attending classes. On Saturdays, I worked if work was available. I maintained that schedule for one and a half years until I paid for my truck.

Again, things got a little easier, but they were still tight. I often reflect on those days and I am thankful for them. Had things been better, I might still be doing construction work and constantly struggling. Fortunately, things were so bad that I was forced to do something else. Around this time, I was going out to dance clubs with my friend, Phillip. We would have some pretty philosophic talks on the way home. One night, I told him some people like us get rich and I didn't understand how that happened. Someone could make $30,000 a year and work for forty years, and that was still only $1.2 million, if one saved his whole paycheck for his entire career. That was a pretty good salary back in those days. Most people are lucky if they can save ten percent (which would only be $120,000), so how in the world did people get rich? Phillip then asked me a life-changing question. "Have you ever heard of *mutual funds*?" I hadn't.

Phillip then explained that a mutual fund was basically a collection of stocks and/or *bonds* that someone else managed for you. All you had to do was put in some money, and it would grow and become larger and larger amounts over time. This was a foreign concept to me. You just gave them money and it increased over time? They weren't like bank CDs that made three to four percent. They made a lot, ten percent or something close to it. Philip then briefly talked about *compound interest*, and it all made much more sense. I still wasn't sure what a stock was, but this conversation had pointed me in the right direction. I knew how to sacrifice, and how to do without things; I knew about delayed gratification. I just didn't know how to make money work for me. How would I find out about this investing thing? As I said earlier, I enjoy finance and investment talk immensely. It is a hobby that has proven very fruitful, and I must admit that I get great satisfaction from helping people. It wasn't something that happened overnight though. By this time in my life, I was nearing the end of college, I was twenty-five years old, and I expected I would eventually have a steadier source of income. I also anticipated that it would be greater than in years past. I decided to find out about these mutual funds and the stock market before I got a good job and steady income stream. I wanted to hit the ground running. This was around

1992 and I knew nothing about the Internet, nor did I know anyone involved in the stock market.

Bottom Line: Hard times often require you to make hard decisions, but for me this led to the seed being planted. This is the first time that I realized there was a way to make money without slaving for it and that money could work for you instead of you working for it.

5

STILL LEARNING

It was 1994 and a couple weeks shy of my twenty-seventh birthday. I married my first wife and we moved to New Mexico. We were both employed and about to make some money. I was a residential building contractor and she was a pharmacist. I was still doing construction, but not as a carpenter anymore. We made a pretty decent living, but it wasn't until the last year of our marriage before we broke into a six-figure combined income. We worked hard and we saved hard. We bought land and invested in mutual funds. And although I had not yet heard of Dave Ramsey, we were already "living like no one else so later we could live like no one else."[22]

We lived in an old ranch house that had two-foot thick adobe walls. The owner, Louis Oliver, was an old rancher who said the previous owners used a grubbing hoe and an axe to cut holes for windows. Louis said the house had originally been built with only portholes; the Indian wars weren't over when the house was built and they were still experiencing Apache raids. There was a sod roof under the tin roof that was nearly rusted through. Our washing machine was on the front porch, and I had to hook it up to a water hose to supply water. We had no central heat or air conditioning. The bathroom had a wood heater, as did the living room. The master bedroom had a wall-mounted propane heater. This was before anyone had wireless cable, so we couldn't pick up any TV stations. My mother-in-law, God bless her, would send us VHS tapes of sitcoms such as Frazier and various other programs.

People thought we were crazy for living such an austere lifestyle, but I'm convinced it's one reason I am where I am today. On the upside, we paid $250 per month in rent, and we had a great landlord. Winter months were cold; the summer weather was warm. I was still driving the old Toyota truck I had bought in college, and my wife had a Dodge Colt she had driven since college. We spent several years doing this and saved a lot of money. The plan was to save diligently for the first seven years and amass about $350,000. Then I figured it would double every seven years (Remember that conversation about compound interest? It took root.). I figured we would retire by the time I was about fifty even if we stopped saving.

We received plenty of unsolicited advice about what we should be doing with money and where we should be spending it though. We tired of all that, but if people think you are crazy, you are probably doing it right. One day my wife came home from work, telling me her coworkers thought we were just throwing money away by renting. They said we should be building equity in a home, and that as a bonus, we could use the mortgage interest we paid as a tax deduction. I decided to get out the calculator and pencil and show her the figures. Keep in mind that mortgage interest rates were over seven percent at the time for a thirty-year fixed mortgage.

I asked her how much her friends paid on their mortgage every month. It was around $1,200. So that meant they roughly borrowed about $150,000 for the home. For the first five years, $150 per month went toward principal. The other $1,050 would be applied towards mortgage interest and escrow. If $1,000 of the monthly payment went to interest, they would get roughly one-third back in taxes. So of the money they spent for the mortgage, $346.50 would be refunded at year's end.

So if we bought a house:

$1,200 spent per month on mortgage

$150 per month x twelve months= $1,800 spent on principal (equity) $1,050 spent on interest, insurance, and taxes per month
We would get about one-third (.33) x $1,050= 346.50 x twelve months = $4,158 back at the end of the year on our tax return

This meant we would spend:

Twelve months x $1,200=$14,400 per year

What would we get in return?

$1,800 in equity + $4,158 tax return = $5,958 in equity
and tax return.

By renting, we spent $250 per month x twelve months = $3,000 per year spent, but we could put $9,000 into investments with the money we saved.
$14,400 spent if we bought a house, of which we would get back $1,800 in equity when we sold and $4,158 back in taxes at the end of the year, for a total of $5,958.

In summary:

By renting, we spent $3,000 per year versus buying, in which we would spend $14,400 per year to get $5,958 = $8,442 spent that we would not recuperate.
$8,442 - $3,000 = $5,442 more to buy than to rent, and we didn't have to pay for home maintenance either. This is an example of *conventional wisdom*. They were well-meaning people who knew just enough to be dangerous when giving unsolicited advice. They had never actually run the numbers. I'm not saying you should dismiss all advice, but if someone says, "You're throwing your money away by renting," at least run some numbers to see whether there is any truth in their statement.
Renting our home, along with a lot of thoughtful sacrifice, put us in a unique position. At this pace, we could stop saving when I was thirty-four and she was thirty. We would retire by the time I was a bit over fifty,

depending on the stock market. We were nearing our goal by the time I was thirty-two, and then our marriage fell apart. It was an unpleasant experience, although I'm sure we are both better off for it. At least we did something right; we saved and invested early. This cannot be overstated. If you are divorced, it may feel like the end of the world. But it really isn't when you consider it from a financial viewpoint. You are not doomed because you are divorced. Does it stink? Absolutely. Can you recover from it? Without a doubt.

If you are young, your greatest ally is time. So get started. We all start from wherever we are. If you are fifty, you obviously have less time than twenty-somethings. But I would offer you the same advice. Don't just think about it; get started. The greatest obstacle I see with friends and family is reluctance to begin. They aren't sure what to do, so they become paralyzed by fear and uncertainty. It's like the saying goes, "When is the best time to plant a tree? Twenty years ago. When is the next best time? Today."

I can assure you it won't get better because you choose to ignore it. It will only be okay because you acted to fix it. I have personally seen the results of people just ignoring it, and it's not pretty. So roll up your sleeves and get to work. My family thought the stock market was the equivalent of gambling, so they gave me no advice other than, "Stay out of the stock market." I was told it was dangerous and you could lose everything you owned.

Ironically, what little people know about investing is what makes it so lucrative in the first place. If people knew how simple it was to make money, I'm sure more people would do it. The reality is that most people do not. The way I started to learn about investing was a painfully slow process. Remember, I knew nothing about the Internet, so I started learning the only way I knew how. I read. I subscribed to *Money* magazine and that was a good place to start. However, the problem was that I knew so little about the jargon used by the writers. I'm convinced most financial writers don't know how little the public understands about stock market vernacular or accounting terms. When I first read EBITDA (Earnings Before Interest, Taxes, Depreciation, and Amortization), and didn't have the Internet to look up the definition, I was staring at that article like a chimpanzee looking at a Rubik's Cube. I had absolutely no idea what that meant, and no one I could ask. I didn't know what a P/E ratio or **dividend** was either.

I finally stumbled upon a highly recommended book called *The Idiot's Guide to Investing*, and it was a great resource. Much of the information covered in this book helped me understand the basics of investing. I'm rather certain none of you started with more of a deficit in financial knowledge than me, so if I can handle it, so can you. Reading this book is a must; it will help you immensely if you don't have a background in finance. For the first several years, I did nothing more than invest in mutual funds. I had read a lot about investing by the time I actually had money to invest, and I was reticent to buy individual stocks. Nearly everyone who was anyone said the best thing to do was to steer clear of individual stocks. This is another example of "conventional wisdom" that hasn't changed much over the years.

So how did I start trading stocks? How did someone like me, without a finance degree and no investment background, figure it out? Well, I was like most people originally, and thought investing in individual stocks was a wild gamble. I figured it would require a lot of time, so I began exclusively with mutual funds.

I liked managed funds because I thought I could get better returns. I would check the five- and ten-year return on funds and make sure the manager had been in place for most of that time. Whenever something would happen, like a fund manager retiring, I would check the new manager's record and find out he seldom had the same track record as his predecessor. I owned a lot of different mutual funds, so the first time I had to sell because of a management change, I opted to reinvest it all in individual stocks. I would put just a few thousand dollars into a stock account, and that would be my "play money."

I had read some Peter Lynch books by now, and this nutty-sounding New Englander was saying regular guys like me could not only make money in the stock market, but that they had an advantage. This was music to my ears. I could have an advantage over the professionals. Mr. Lynch maintained that if a guy was able to keep a clear head and make rational decisions, he could buy stock in small companies that were often of no interest to mutual funds. This allowed the little guy like me to move in and out of stocks with much more ease than the big guys. The idea of buying what you knew about sounded like a novel concept; an experiment I definitely wanted to try. So many experts were saying it was folly (conventional wisdom). I didn't want to risk too much money in the "Wall Street casino," so I played small and kept the serious money in mutual funds.

What I learned from that experiment is this: I got better returns from the individual stocks, and I didn't have to pay a *front-end load* (basically a sales commission). I did have to pay a small broker's fee but it was insignificant. I also had a smaller tax liability because I didn't trade as frequently as fund managers. My stocks seemed to perform better than my mutual funds, and I enjoyed it. I had bought my mutual funds based on the fund manager's track record. When that manager was preparing to retire or leave, I would sell it and move that money into my stock account. It didn't take long before I had moved all of my money out of mutual funds and into individual stocks. By now, I held no money in mutual funds other than what was offered through my employer's retirement plan (individual stocks were not available). As an aside, virtually no company-sponsored retirement accounts will permit you to buy individual stocks.

Bottom line: start wherever you are in life. The most important thing is just to start. If you wait until everything is perfect before starting down your path to financial freedom, you will never *begin*.

6

PRIORITIES:
WHY MORE PEOPLE
AREN'T WEALTHY

AT A TIME WHEN knowledge and know-how are at everyone's fingertips, why aren't more people wealthy? Why do people continue to struggle in retirement? While I think this question requires a multi-faceted answer, I believe there are a few similar stumbling blocks for most people. One is that people think they are *too busy* to become wealthy. They become overly distracted with day-to-day stuff; they work too many hours, spending what little leftover time they have at sporting events and school activities. When they finally get through the door after a long day, they are exhausted.

Becoming wealthy is *not* more important than spending time with your kids. But if you *make* time to work on Fantasy football draft choices and post about your favorite football team on Facebook, then I would argue you have time to learn how to become wealthy. Perhaps you spend the weekend riding motorcycles, camping, watching football, or going out drinking with friends. There *is* time, but you just spend it on other activities. I have had conversations with several of my friends who are sports fanatics. They can quote RBIs for a player from thirty years ago, they know who won the World Series every year for the last ten years, and which teams won every Super

Bowl ever played. Yet if I asked them about a **Roth IRA** or how much they will need to live comfortably in retirement, they are clueless.

While I don't share the same enthusiasm for sports, I believe there's nothing wrong with being passionate about a hobby. The problem simply lies in where most people place their priorities. In fact, it's safe to say that most people don't prioritize at all. As Zig Ziglar says, "If you aim at nothing, you will hit it every time."[23]

I'm not saying that you have to adopt my priorities, but can we all agree that not eating dog food upon retirement is more important than knowing who will be the top quarterback in the NFL this year?

One of the big tenets of Ramsey's message is telling your money what to do, rather than letting it get away and being clueless about what happened to it. The same is true of time. If you wander around aimlessly, not doing anything productive, you lose that time; you'll never get it back. Time will not wait until you are ready; it will move on and you will get older. You will either be more prepared for the future or you will not be prepared at all. The difference in these outcomes is almost entirely dependent on your behavior. Yes, some things will happen beyond your control. However, most outcomes are heavily influenced by your behavior.

For instance, you will undoubtedly experience health problems as you age. However, if you are thirty-five years old, forty pounds overweight, lead a very sedentary lifestyle, and develop heart disease or diabetes, there is a very real possibility that it could have been avoided. If you spent your rent money at a bar or borrowed from your retirement fund to go on vacation, you are also at fault.

So what is the first step in prioritizing? That first step is choosing what is important. Make a list of your priorities and spend some time thinking about what you write down. Be honest with yourself. This may sound ridiculously simple, yet most people don't actually know what they value besides the obvious things like family and health. Are there other things that hold importance? What about retirement, kids' college funds, or your friends? Sit down and decide what's important; make a conscious decision where you will spend your time and effort.

> **Wherever your treasure is, there the desires of your heart will also be.**
>
> —Matthew 6:21

My priority list is not very long, but I try to make a conscious effort to follow it daily:

1. **God/Faith**
   Pray, read the Bible, help someone.
2. **Family**
   Call/connect; spend quality time together.
3. **Friends**
   Call/connect; spend quality time together.
4. **Health**
   Eat well; exercise regularly.
5. **Wealth**
   Build retirement funds; build college funds.
6. **Work**
   Job satisfaction; salary increase

I don't aim to preach or force my priorities on you. I will also tell you that I don't always accomplish my priorities daily, but I do make a conscious effort every day to pursue things in this order. Friends are categorized separately on my list. Some are as close as family and others are work acquaintances. But they all fall somewhere on this spectrum. My faith is most important. I know a lot of people don't like Mr. Ramsey because of his religious references, but he doesn't seem to care and I don't either. You will notice that my family is more important than my own health, but my health is still important. Here's why: if I'm unhealthy, I will spend a lot less time with my family. Wealth is lower on my list because if I don't have my family or my health, then wealth is nearly useless. I might still need money

41

to survive, but if I had a choice between wealth and my family, I would choose my family every time.

You will also notice that work is the last thing on my list. This is not to say that work is unimportant. Obviously, it's how I have saved money to build wealth in the first place and I enjoy my work most of the time. However, it is just a means of supporting other things on my list. I have known far too many co-workers who have spent years working sixteen-hour days trying to get a promotion that would increase their pay just ten percent each year. While that is a nice pay increase, what could they achieve instead by spending one to two hours each day increasing their knowledge about finance and investing? Just that simple change would increase their net worth by far more than a ten percent pay increase, and they would spend far less time achieving it. Also keep in mind that the amount made from investments will eventually not only be greater than a ten percent pay increase, but also greater than an entire paycheck.

If you are married, get your spouse involved in the priority list process. I can't say this enough: *you need to share goals with your spouse.* I see people who struggle and fight over money all the time because one spouse believes the other is trying to control or manipulate them. They feel as if they are being treated like a child because one wants to save and the other wants to live it up now. The spender may go so far as maxing out credit cards they have hidden from their saver spouse.

You need to share your goals with your spouse.

The easiest way to avoid this type of mess is by ensuring "buy-in" for both you *and* your spouse. I got my wife on board when we agreed that upon paying off our mortgage, she could quit her job and stay home with our children. She was in up to her neck, and worked like crazy to reach this goal.

If you want to minimize fights, make goals that appeal to both of you, even if it is for different reasons. Others have allowed their marriages to crumble while chasing a promotion, then end up spending far more than their pay raise to shell out alimony and child support. And even *that* is nothing compared to the pain caused by divorce. Why place a job in front of your family?

Like Papaw Franklin, others don't value their health until it's too late. When these workaholics are forced to retire due to age or health, they are completely lost. They don't have a family, they don't have their job, and they don't have their health. Instead of pursuing their own interests, they look for another job because they are bored, lonely, or too broke to enjoy retirement. Don't do this; don't lose sight of what is important. The best way to do this is to slow down long enough to decide what you value, then refocus your priorities accordingly. We all have our own value systems, so use this exercise to clarify your priorities.

Many seem to have no concept of the "work-reward" correlation either. When I was a carpenter, co-workers would tell me they had no interest in working Saturdays or overtime shifts because their wives took that money anyway. What was the point? I guess I always felt like there was one. I remember doing construction work in the hot sun or cold winter and puzzling over doing something with my friends. I would consider how much work I had to perform to pay for a movie. Here was my thought process: "Okay, it's $8 for a ticket and $2 for a Coke. That's $10. If I had to spend three hours in the hot sun digging a footing to earn this money, is it worth it?"

The answer was often "no" for me. I think most people really believe they are going to be poor for a lifetime, so what difference does hustling really make? They have learned helplessness. How many people do you know who think nothing of dropping $5 for their daily Starbucks latte, but don't have extra money to contribute to their child's college fund? One of the dumbest things I have seen is people buying designer shoes for a child who is too young to walk, and then telling me they can't afford to save anything for the child's education.

Or maybe you have acquaintances who love taking lavish vacations every year, but they can't afford to fund a retirement IRA. Again, it all comes back to priorities. The power to choose your own priorities is one of your greatest responsibilities. Choose wisely.

43

Another stumbling block for most people is their lack of understanding. They don't know what a ***compounding factor*** is or why it's important to start saving and investing early. I will discuss three different scenarios. Most people follow the first plan below, if they have any plan at all. We were told to get an education, work hard, make lots of money and save a bunch of it, and everything would work out well. While all these are important, they are only half of the story.

> ***The power to choose your own priorities is one of your greatest responsibilities. Choose wisely.***

Scenario #1

First, let's assume that you are going to average a $40,000 yearly gross salary for a forty-year career (ages twenty-five to sixty-five). We will leave out inflation, pay raises, and taxes just to simplify the math. We will also assume that you save twenty percent of your gross income yearly ($8,000). This leaves you with $32,000 to live on. You do not invest the proceeds, you just put it in a non-interest-bearing savings account because that's really safe. That means that at the end of your career when you turn sixty-five, you would have $320,000 in savings. This means if you kept the same lifestyle, spending $32,000 a year, you would be completely broke by age seventy-five. Wow! It took forty years to save it, and only ten years to spend it all. Is this your plan? Most folks seem to live by this scenario. But now you can see that even solely saving isn't sustainable. If you live long enough, you will have absolutely nothing.

Here is the math:

> $40,000/year salary x 20% savings = $8,000/year saved
>
> $8,000/year x 40 years = $320,000 total for retirement

Savings/Investments Before Retirement

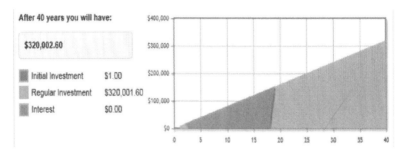

After 40 years you will have:

$320,002.60

Initial Investment	$1.00
Regular Investment	$320,001.60
Interest	$0.00

Spending/Investments After Retirement

Spending $32,000 per year in retirement x 10 years = $320,000 and it's all gone.

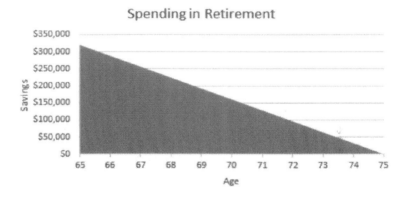

Spending in Retirement

Scenario #2

Let's look at a second scenario. We will use the same salary example ($40,000). Career length (forty years) and retirement age (sixty-five) also stay the same. The only difference is this: on the day he turns sixty-five, this lucky guy suddenly learns how to invest. Instead of keeping his $320,000 in a non-interest-bearing savings account, he instead purchases an index mutual fund that averages a ten percent return per year. At this rate, his $320,000 will produce an extra $32,000 per year. His annual retirement income is still the same as when he was working. The best part is that after ten years, he still has $320,000 in his retirement account. He has been able to maintain the same comfortable lifestyle for ten years, and still has the same amount of money with which he started.

Here's the math:

$40,000/year salary x 20% savings = $8,000/year
$8,000/year x 40 years = $320,000 total for retirement
$320,000 x 10% return = $32,000/year
retirement income
$32,000 x 10 years = $320,000 and still has $320,000 in
his account

Savings/Investments Before Retirement

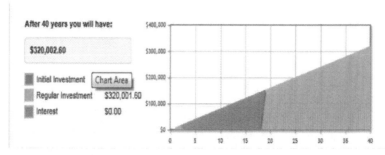

Spending/Investments After Retirement

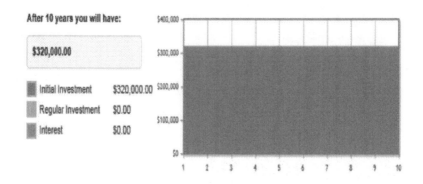

Scenario #3

Let's look at a third scenario. We will assume the same salary, the same rate of savings, and the same career span. However, instead of putting his money in a non-interest-bearing checking account, our friend starts investing at twenty-five. He puts $666.67 per month ($8,000 per year) in an index mutual fund. When he reaches sixty-five, he will have $3,729,756 in his retirement.

> $32,000 salary x 20% savings = $8,000/year
> $8,000 x 40 years = $320,000 invested
> $666.67 per month x 12 months = $8,000 per year
> $8,000 per year earning 10% per year compounded for
>   40 years = $3,729,756
> $3,729,756 x 10 % per year = $372,975 per year

The only change in each of these scenarios is the age at which our retiree learns how to make money work for him. Everything else is the same.

Savings/Investment Account Before Retirement

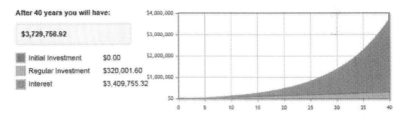

This is an illustration of scenarios 1 and 2 versus scenario 3 upon retiring. The savings rate is the same in each scenario, but in scenarios 1 and 2 you retire with $320,000. In scenario 3, because you start investing immediately, you retire with just shy of $4,000,000.

Saving for Retirement vs. Investing for Retirement

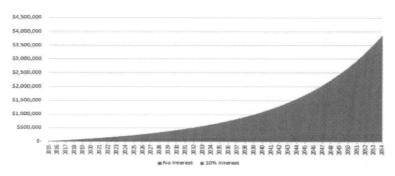

Let's review:

Scenario #1

Retire with $320,000 at sixty-five years old, and live on $32,000 yearly. At seventy-five, $0 and broke.

Scenario #2

Retire with $320,000 at sixty-five years old, and live on $32,000 per year from now on. He would still have $320,000 for the rest of his life.

Scenario #3

Retire at sixty-five years old with almost $4,000,000; live on $372,000 (almost 12 times as much as the other two scenarios) per year from now on, and have almost $4,000,000 for the rest of his life.

Again, the only difference between living the rest of your life wealthy versus being broke is when you learn to make money work for you.

In the first two scenarios, why is there such a discrepancy? I know we said make money work for you, but what exactly is responsible for going from $320,000 in the bank to $4 million? The answer is compound interest. We hear the term constantly, but what does it really mean?

> *Compound interest is the eighth wonder of the world. He who understands it, earns it. He who doesn't, pays it.*
>
> —Albert Einstein

The addition of interest to the principal sum of a loan or deposit is called *compounding*. Compound interest is interest on interest. It is the result of reinvesting interest, rather than paying it out. That interest in the next period is then earned on the principal sum plus previously accumulated interest. Compound interest is standard in finance and economics.

> *Compound interest is the most powerful force in the universe.*
>
> —Albert Einstein

Do you understand compounding? Let's see. If you were offered one penny that would double in value every day for thirty days or $1 million, which would you take? If you chose $1 million, either you are really rushed or you do not understand compounding. The penny doubling every day for thirty days would be $5,368,709.12. How can that be possible? It is the miracle of compounding. There is an Indian folk story that goes as follows.

The Grain of Rice Fable[24]

Long ago in India, there lived a raja who believed he was wise and fair, as a raja should be. The people in his province were rice farmers. The raja decreed that everyone must give nearly all their rice to him. "I will store the rice safely," the raja promised the people, "so that in time of famine, everyone will have rice to eat, and no one will go hungry." Each year, the raja's rice collectors gathered nearly all the people's rice and carried it away to the royal storehouses.

For many years, the rice grew well. The people gave nearly all their rice to the raja, and the storehouses were always full. But the people were left with only enough rice to get by. Then one year the rice grew badly and there was famine and hunger. The people had no rice to give to the raja, and they had no rice to eat. The raja's ministers implored him, "Your Highness, let us open the royal storehouses and give the rice to the people, as you promised." "No," cried the raja. How do I know how long the famine will last? I must have the rice for myself. Promise or no promise, a raja must not go hungry."

Time went on, and the people grew more and more hungry. But the raja would not give out the rice. One day, the raja ordered a feast for himself and his court, as it seemed to him, a raja should now and then, even when there is famine. A servant led an elephant from a royal storehouse to the palace, carrying two full baskets of rice. A village girl named Rani saw that a trickle of rice was falling from one of the baskets. Quickly she jumped up and walked along beside the elephant, catching the falling rice in her skirt. She was clever, and she began to plan.

At the palace, a guard cried, "Halt, thief. Where are you going with that rice?" "I am not a thief," Rani replied. "This rice fell from one of the baskets, and I am returning it now to the raja."

When the raja heard about Rani's good deed, he asked his ministers to bring her before him. "I wish to reward you for returning what belongs to me," the raja said to Rani. "Ask me for anything, and you shall have it."

"Your highness," said Rani, "I do not deserve any reward at all. But if you wish, you may give me one grain of rice."

"Only one grain of rice?" exclaimed the raja. "Surely you will allow me to reward you more plentifully, as a raja should."

"Very well," said Rani. "If it pleased Your Highness, you may reward me in this way. Today, you will give me a single grain of rice. Then, each day for thirty days you will give me double the rice you gave me the day before. Thus, tomorrow you will give me two grains of rice, the next day four grains of rice, and so on for thirty days."

"This seems to be a modest reward," said the raja. "But you shall have it."

And Rani was presented with a single grain of rice. The next day, Rani was presented with two grains of rice. And the following day, Rani was presented with four grains of rice.

Priorities: Why More People Aren't Wealthy

On the ninth day, Rani was presented with 256 grains of rice. She had received in all, five hundred and eleven grains of rice, enough for only a small handful. "This girl is honest, but not very clever," thought the raja. "She would have gained more rice by keeping what fell into her skirt."

On the twelfth day, Rani received 2,048 grains of rice, about four handfuls. On the thirteenth day, she received 4,096 grains of rice, enough to fill a bowl. On the sixteenth day, Rani was presented with a bag containing 32,768 grains of rice. All together she had enough rice for two bags. "This doubling up adds up to more rice than I expected," thought the raja. "But surely her reward won't amount to much more."

On the twenty-first day, she received 1,048,576 grains of rice, enough to fill a basket. On the twenty-fourth day, Rani was presented with 8,388,608 grains of rice–enough to fill eight baskets, which were carried to her by eight royal deer. On the twenty-seventh day, thirty-two brahma bulls were needed to deliver sixty-four baskets of rice. The raja was deeply troubled. "One grain of rice has grown very great indeed," he thought. "But I shall fulfill the reward to the end, as a raja should."

On the twenty-ninth day, Rani was presented with the contents of two royal storehouses. On the thirtieth and final day, two hundred and fifty-six elephants crossed the province, carrying the contents of the last four royal storehouses—536,870,912 grains of rice.

Altogether, Rani had received more than *one billion grains of rice*! The raja had no more rice to give. "And what will you do with this rice," said the raja with a sigh, "now that I have none?"

"I shall give it to all the hungry people," said Rani, "and I shall leave a basket of rice for you, too, if you promise from now on to take only as much rice as you need."

"I promise," said the raja. And for the rest of his days, the raja was truly wise and fair, as a raja should be.

The same principle applies to your retirement money. It all depends on how early you start and how often you can make it double. This miracle of compounding is why the money you save can eventually become insignificant. For example, let's say you save $1,250 per month. That ends up being $15,000 per year. If you put this in an investment vehicle (such as an index mutual fund) that makes ten percent per year, it will take right at five years for you to have $100,000 in that account. If you continue putting that same $1,250 per month in your account, you will accumulate $262,000 in another five years. This is all from compounding.

At this stage of the game, your $262,000 will produce $26,200 in profits, already dwarfing your $15,000 yearly contribution. This cycle will get shorter each time your investments gain another $100,000. It will take you five years for your first $100,000, just over three for your second $100,000, and just over two for you to reach $300,000. By the time you reach $1 million, your investment should be returning $100,000 per year, making your $15,000 yearly contribution seem rather insignificant by comparison.

> Year 1 $15,000
> Year 2 $15,000 saved + $15,000 from previous year +
> $1,500 interest= $31,500 total
> Year 3 $15,000 saved + $31,500 from previous year
> +$3,150 interest earned = $49,650 total

At that point, your $300,000 is making $30,000 plus the $15,000 you are saving. It takes less than two years for you to reach $400,000. By the time you reach $850,000, which, at a ten percent return makes $85,000 per year added to the $15,000 you save, you are increasing your holdings by $100,000 every year. Each year the amount you have working for you increases, as does the return on your investment.

Here's another way of looking at it. There are 365 days in a year and you are making $100,000 per year just in investment returns by the time you hit one million dollars. That means every day you are making $273.97 with no additional effort. When you are sleeping, it's making money; when you are on vacation, it's working for you. When you are resting, your money is hard at work producing for you. The best part is that it's not taxed unless you choose to sell it. Every bit not paid to you in dividends or sold off is still working for you. This amount will increase every year; it just gets bigger and works harder.

It may take you twenty years to make your first million, but each time the turnaround is significantly shorter until you make your second million and third million. The first million takes twenty years, the second takes a bit over six years, and the third million will take right at four years. Each time it gets shorter and shorter. By this time, your investments have reached $3 million and should produce about $300,000 every year without you adding a penny.

If you started on this plan when you were twenty-five years old, by the time you arrive at fifty-five years old, you should have nearly $3 million in investments. If you stopped contributing any savings at this point, you would still easily have over $7 million by the time you retired at age sixty-five! If you manage your own stocks and they return even a percentage point or two higher, you will have much more than that. The key is starting early. I call this the investment snowball, much like Ramsey's debt snowball, because it works both ways.

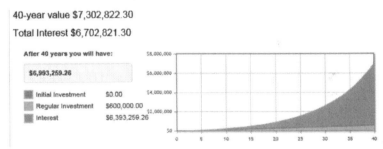

Two things should jump out at you: one is that you only saved $600,000. The rest is interest on interest on interest, the power of compounding. The second is how steep the graph becomes at the end as the compounding really kicks in. Each successive million is made in a shorter span of time. When Buffett turned sixty, his net worth was $3.8 billion. Now at eighty-five, he's worth $58.5 billion. That means that ninety-four percent of his wealth was created after the age of sixty.[25]

Also keep in mind that you essentially cut your wealth in half for every seven years you delay getting started. This is due to the Rule of 72 and the long-term market return of ten percent. Every 7.2 years, your wealth should double. Every seven years you wait, it cuts that amount in half. Again, when I say wealth building is a life-long process and shouldn't be rushed, I merely mean you should take the time to educate yourself. Don't delay in saving. From the example below, we see that a one-time investment of $1,000 in an investment vehicle that produces a ten percent annual return is about $45,000 after forty years. It is only $23,000 after thirty-three years. This means that if you hit the work force at twenty-five, and place $1,000 in an index mutual fund, you would have twice as much as if you did the same thing at thirty-two years of age. It would reduce to around $12,000 if you waited until age thirty-nine. Hopefully now you see that you simply cannot afford to wait. If you delay, you will pay an enormous price.

If you waited until you were thirty-two years old and invested the same $1,000, it would reduce by nearly half to just $23,225.20.

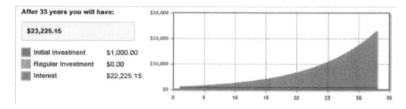

If you waited until thirty-nine, that same $1,000 invested would cut in half the amount you would retire with by $11,918. Each time you wait seven years, you cut your retirement in half.

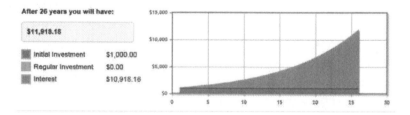

Priorities: Why More People Aren't Wealthy

I don't minimize hard work. It is important; it's how we get ahead and how we contribute. But working is one of the least efficient ways to build wealth. Look at it in a certain light. It's as if you had to be in a place two hundred miles from where you are, and the only way to get there was to walk. Flying would have you there in an hour and a half, depending on the plane. It would be the most efficient method of travel. A car would have you there in a bit over three hours. A bicycle would have you there, but it might take a couple of days. Walking might take over three weeks. I would never suggest you just sit down just because your only available mode of transportation were your feet. I would instead tell you to get moving. Making money is the same way. Working may be the least efficient way to produce wealth, but if that's all you have, then that's what you must do.

For example, if you start saving for a bicycle or other mode of transportation, you will be better off the next time you need to make the trip. However, if you spend all your money eating out or getting massages, you must expend just as much effort as you did the last time when making the trek. If you save and invest, eventually you can buy a bicycle or car. Then you can save and invest even more, eventually buying an airplane. Then, that three-week trip turns into an hour and a half. It all depends on your behavior.

Working is one of the least efficient ways to build wealth.

Bottom Line: Make your money work for you. You worked hard for it, so make it work just as hard for you. Why? It is the difference between you being broke at seventy-five years old, or living a very comfortable lifestyle with millions of dollars in the bank for the rest of your life. Saving is only half of the formula. The other half is making money work for you.

7

TAXES

I WANT TO REITERATE a few points before we go deeply into the tax talk. Firstly, I am not a **CPA**, nor am I offering tax advice here. The illustrations are ball-park estimates and are not exact. Many tax professionals will not give you an exact number if you ask them how much in taxes you will owe, usually because of liability purposes and because even these professionals cannot agree on your tax liability. Consequently, they are reticent to give you an estimate. Therefore, I will not argue about the exact accuracy of my numbers because even the experts cannot agree.

To better understand taxes, we need to delve ever so slightly into our tax system. Most "experts" stay away from the subject, which is another reason people understand so little about it. But for the sake of educating ourselves, we are going to do our best to address this complicated monstrosity.[26]

Have you ever watched a young person receive their first real paycheck? I say real because many kids who pitched hay, built fence, or performed back-breaking labor much like me weren't paid for it. So I'm talking about a real, bona-fide job where they get a paycheck from an employer. Indeed, the magic moment arrives when they discover their time is worth something to someone else. When they see that first check written out for substantially less than the actual wage they worked hard for, they usually protest at the unfairness of it all. Finally, they walk away in disgusted disbelief. Such is the beginning of many careers. It tickles me, but perhaps I'm a little sadistic. I'm amused because when taxpayers complain about some of the ridiculous expenditures of the government, these are the same people who tell you to get it over it. Before I paid taxes, I was one of these people. Yet it becomes a big deal when it personally affects you. I cannot help but smile whenever this revelation occurs.

Undoubtedly, the federal tax system is extremely complicated. Why else would we hire accountants whose income is earned solely by determining someone's yearly tax liability? Whenever you can take your tax information to five different tax "professionals" and each one offers a unique assessment of your tax liability, you can rest assured it's a convoluted, bureaucratic, red-tape-filled mess.[27] I read about a study from *Money* magazine in which forty-six different tax professionals with five different programs had the exact same tax information, and every one of them came back with a different estimate on how much would be owed in taxes. Their computing inconsistencies ranged thousands of dollars: from $34,240 to $68,912. Many wealthy people claim to support our current tax system, yet these same people hire armies of accountants and lawyers to reduce the amount of taxes they pay out.

Most people are ignorant about taxes. As you already know, I'm no expert. Who can be when the code changes constantly? Did you know that many foreign banks will not accept United States customers anymore because the tax reporting requirements are so strenuous and formidable? It's no wonder people are relinquishing United States citizenship in record numbers to escape excessive taxes. Perhaps you've also noticed that many companies are moving overseas. The U.S. government suspects trillions of dollars are hidden in offshore accounts just to escape taxes. Why do I bring this up? To address the possibility of avoiding some of these taxes, of course. Let's get something straight first. There is a difference between tax avoidance and tax evasion.

Tax avoidance is the legitimate minimizing of taxes, using methods approved by the ***Internal Revenue Service (IRS)***. Businesses avoid taxes by taking all legitimate deductions and by sheltering income from taxes setting up employee retirement plans and other means, all legal and under the IRS or state tax codes.

Tax evasion, on the other hand, is the illegal practice of not paying taxes by not reporting income, reporting expenses not legally allowed, or by not paying taxes owed.

2016 tax brackets (for taxes due April 17, 2017)

Tax rate	Single filers	Married filing jointly or qualifying widow/widower	Married filing separately	Head of household
10%	Up to $9,275	Up to $18,550	Up to $9,275	Up to $13,250
15%	$9,276 to $37,650	$18,551 to $75,300	$9,276 to $37,650	$13,251 to $50,400
25%	$37,651 to $91,150	$75,301 to $151,900	$37,651 to $75,950	$50,401 to $130,150
28%	$91,151 to $190,150	$151,901 to $231,450	$75,951 to $115,725	$130,151 to $210,800
33%	$190,151 to $413,350	$231,451 to $413,350	$115,726 to $206,675	$210,801 to $413,350
35%	$413,351 to $415,050	$413,351 to $466,950	$206,676 to $233,475	$413,351 to $441,000
39.6%	$415,051 or more	$466,951 or more	$233,476 or more	$441,001 or more

Chart courtesy of www.bankrate.com/finance/taxes/tax-brackets.aspx

I am not advising anyone to break the law by evading taxes, but I encourage you to at least learn the tax code basics. Firstly, understand there is an **income tax rate** and a **long-term capital gains tax rate**. The United States has a graduated tax system. Here is a basic illustration.

Let's assume you make $100,000 this year. This means that if you are single, you are taxed at a ten percent rate up until you hit $9,275. Then the portion between $9,276 and $37,650 is taxed at fifteen percent. The next portion from $37,651 to $91,150 is taxed at twenty-five percent. Finally, the portion from $91,151 to $100,000 would be taxed at twenty-eight percent.

The math would look something like this:

$$\$9,275 \times .10 = \$927.50$$
$$\$37,650 - \$9,275 = \$28,375 \times .15 = \$4,256.25$$
$$150 - \$37,650 = \$53,500 \times .25 = \$13,375$$
$$ - \$91,151 = \$9,275 \times .28 = \$2,597$$
$$d = \$21,155.75$$

Taxes

Your effective federal income tax rate would be about twenty-one per-cent. What should jump out at you is this: The first $9,275 you earned was taxed at ten percent, so the taxes on it are $927.50. The last $9,275 you earned was taxed at twenty-eight percent, and you paid $2,597 on the same amount of income! Remember, this is federal tax only; it doesn't include state taxes or social security. The only difference is the income bracket in which the IRS categorized the money; this is referred to as a marginal tax rate. This results in you paying nearly three times the tax amount.

A ***marginal tax rate*** is the amount of tax paid on an additional dollar of income. This method of taxation aims to fairly tax individuals based upon their earnings, with low-income earners being taxed at a lower rate than higher income earners. Someone who makes $100,000 per year has a higher marginal tax rate than someone making $25,000 in that same year.

However, the marginal tax rate does not increase for one's entire income, just each dollar over a certain threshold (referenced in the example above). Suppose you pay ten percent of your income up to $25,000, and twenty percent thereafter. (These are not actual rates; I just used the percentages to simplify the math.) The taxpayer making $25,001 does not suddenly have to pay twenty percent of his/her entire income, only on the $1 over $25,000. This means they owe ten percent of $25,000 ($2,500) and twenty percent of the $1 over that (or $0.20). All things being equal, this taxpayer owes $2,500.20 in taxes. We also must remember Social Security tax. If you are self-employed, you pay 12.4 percent in **SSI** and 2.9 percent in Medicare tax, totaling 15.3 percent for the Self-Employed Contributions Act (SECA). If you work for someone else, you split this amount. This means you pay 7.65 percent and your employer pays the other half.

You're probably thinking you can't get out of taxes at this point. Yet that is only partially true. You can do what many wealthy people do; earn money through investments and pay a capital gains tax.

Unearned income from stocks, versus the income most of us earn from our jobs, is taxed as capital gains. There are long-term and short-term cap-ital gains taxes. Long-term includes assets held longer than 365 days, while short-term is considered assets held less than 365 days. The highest capital gains tax rate (for now) on long-term investments is just fifteen percent, unless you make over $200,000 in yearly income. As an aside, if you are making over $100,000 a year, you really need to hire an accountant (CPA) to file your taxes. As I stated earlier, the U.S. tax code is a nightmare; why not leave that mess to a professional? Again, I want you to realize the importance of legally keeping as much of your money as possible. How much you keep heavily depends on how you earn it.

I discuss this topic with a lot of people, but very few people who work for a living understand it. Why? Because:

1. The majority of people who work for a living don't delve into stocks, and
2. Our tax system is so complicated very few people can understand it without reading up on it daily.

It's no wonder, with terms such as *earned income vs. unearned income*, a *graduated tax system* with *marginal rates vs. effective rates, long-term capital gains vs. short-term capital gains*. Finally, we have *tax avoidance vs. tax evasion* (which were both defined earlier in this chapter).

This is before we even begin to probe into Roth IRAs, *Traditional IRAs*, 401(k)s, *Simplified Employee Pension Plans (SEP)*, and all the complicated rules surrounding them. I believe most of this is by design; if the rules are so complicated that what you owe becomes subjective, then you just give up and pay the maximum amount to avoid trouble with the IRS. These rules change regularly, and CPAs are required to attend continuing education courses just to keep up with the changes. It's no wonder that working-class people throw their hands in the air and just give up.

I have gone in to detail, but this is what I hope you realize as a result: keeping your money is imperative to building wealth. Let's revisit our previous example assuming you make about $100,000 per year. Let's also assume that you wanted to increase your retirement savings, so you obtain a part-time job that earns you an additional $10,000 per year. The math would look something like this on your regular income of $100,426:

$9,275 x .10 = $927.50
$37,650 - $9,275 = $28,375 x .15 = $4,256.25
$91,150 - $37,650= 53,500 x .25 = $13,375
$100,426 - $91,151= $9,275 x .28 = $2,597
Total taxes paid = $21,155.75

With the extra $10,000 it looks like this:

$9,275 x .10 = $927.50
$37,650 - 9,275 = $28,375 x .15 = $4,256.25
$91,150 - $37,650 = $53,500 x .25 = $13,375
$110,426 - $91,151= $19,275 x .28 = $5,397

In addition, you would pay social security and Medicare taxes that range from 7.65 to 15.3 percent, depending on whether you work for an employer yourself.

Total taxes paid = $23,955.75 before **Supplemental Security Income (SSI)** and **Medicare**

Total 1: $21,155.75
Total 2: $23,955.75

You pay an additional $2,800 in federal taxes because you took a second job. The extra income gets taxed at your top marginal rate, in this case twenty-eight percent. That means you would only keep $7,200 after paying taxes.

Keep in mind you would still have to pay state income tax (if your state requires it). I live in New Mexico, so that costs me an additional 4.9 percent. I would also have to pay social security taxes; presently, that is 7.65 percent if I am working for someone else.

$10,000 x .049 = $245 (state taxes)
$10,000 x .0765 = $765 (social security taxes)

The Money Talk

$7,200 - $245 = $6,710 - $76 5= $5,945 (remaining
after state and federal taxes)

For now, let's look at how working a second job ($10,000 per year) results in only $5,945 left over after state and federal taxes. If you are self-employed, you will pay double the amount of social security tax because employers pay half your social security tax. However, if you are a business owner, you are also your employer. That would further reduce your earnings from $5,945 to $5,180. This results in you keeping just over $0.50 on every dollar you earned. That's a bleak picture, isn't it?

Let's consider another possibility. Imagine you put your money in individual stocks and you didn't sell a single thing this year, but your stock value ended the year up ten percent. Let's say you had $100,000 in your stock account and you made a ten percent average long-term market return. You don't sell your stock; you just continue to let it work for you (it's a company you love with great growth prospects for years to come). Here is the best part: you don't owe *any* social security tax on capital gains even when you do sell it.

Let's look at the math:

$100,000 invested x 10 percent average return
= $10,000
Your **net worth** went up by $10,000.

Keep in mind that this is just a long-term average, so it could be lower or higher. However, over the years, this is what it *should* average. This $10,000 increase in net worth is what we call *unrealized gain*. It is also known as a paper profit. How much tax do you owe on the paper profit? Zero, zilch, nada, nothing. And that, my friends, is referred to as *tax avoidance*. It's perfectly legal, and virtually all wealthy people do it.

If you made the $10,000 working, and you have a regular income of $100,000 per year, you would have less than $6,700 left to invest elsewhere. If you had a $100,000 income and you made the $10,000 with investments, this is referred to as *unearned income*. This means you would still have the entire $10,000 *working for you.*

Working vs. Investing

When you work for it, you keep less than $6,700. But when you make $10,000 through investing, the money keeps working for you. You might be asking, *What happens when I sell? Won't I owe taxes?* The answer is yes. If you hold the investment for less than one year, you owe short-term capital gains tax. This means you owe roughly the same tax amount as if you earned it through a job.

However, if you hold the investment for one year and one day, you will typically owe fifteen percent in federal taxes. Again, I live in New Mexico, so I would owe 2.45 (the first half of capital gains are tax exempt in New Mexico) percent in state taxes (fifteen percent federal + 2.45 percent state =17.45 percent total) and no social security or Medicare tax, versus 32.9 percent if I had earned it through a job. Let's say I kept that $10,000 in the stock market for the next 21.6 years without selling because I bought a wonderful stock. Then let's assume it grew at ten percent per year, the rate of the general market. This means it would turn over *three* times using the Rule of 72.

Rule of 72 – If you divide seventy-two by the interest rate or rate of return you expect to get from an investment, it will take that number of years for the investment to double.

Most people cannot do logarithmic functions in their heads, but they can divide seventy-two by ten and get 7.2, which is almost the same thing. The Rule of 72 works best for interest rates between six percent and ten percent. It's accuracy wanes as you stray from that range. However, you can still use this as a rule of thumb. This means $10,000 would double to $20,000 in seven years. That $20,000 would double to $40,000 in fourteen years, and then you would hit $80,000 in twenty-one years (assuming ten percent return).

If I took the $6,700 earned from working and put it in the stock market, it would double to $13,400 in seven years. That $13,400 would turn into

$26,800 in fourteen years, and then hit $53,600 in twenty-one years. You would now owe long-term capital gains in either scenario (you held it longer than one year, remember?).

Let's look at the numbers:

Money Earned Working versus Money Earned Investing

$53,600 x 17.45 percent taxes = $9,353.20
$80,000 x 17.45 percent = $13,960.00 total taxes paid
Realized gain is $53,600 - $9,353.20 = $44,246.80
$80,000 - $13,960.00 = $66,040.00
Earned by working: $44,246.80
Earned by investing: $66,040.00

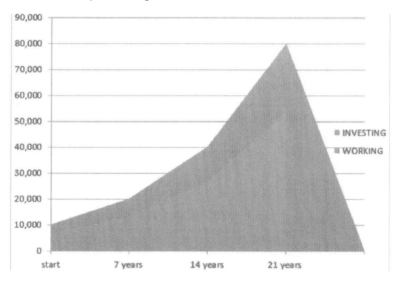

Many people want to start small businesses to get wealthy; I much admire these people. However, when you expend money and effort in one area, you will have less time and money to expend elsewhere. My point is you will almost always make more money with your brain than with your back.

Taxes

I thought long and hard about ways to get wealthy. Starting a business has come to mind on more than one occasion. While I'm not dismissing the idea, I would caution you to ensure it is worth your time and effort. I myself have considered various businesses such as buying and renovating a foreclosure to sell for a profit.

Here was my problem. If I bought the house for $100,000, spent another $10,000 fixing it up, and spent eight hours working every Saturday for six months, I would have $110,000 plus 200 hours of my time in the house. Then I would have to consider closing costs and realtor fees. I might have $120,000 tied up for an entire year. If I sold the house for $132,000, I would make $12,000 in profit. I would then owe taxes on these gains.

> $100,000 house price
> $10,000 materials
> $10,000 realtor and closing fees
> $120,000 total invested
> $132,000 sale price - $120,000 invested = $12,000 profit
> $12,000 gain / 200 hours worked = $60/hour

Awesome, right? Well yes, but if you weren't borrowing the money you were using to buy the house and you had invested that $120,000 in the stock market over that one-year period, averaging a ten percent return, (let's say in an ***index mutual fund***) it would have made you $12,000. If you left the money in the mutual fund or stocks, you wouldn't owe taxes on it either. You could spend six months working all day every Saturday, or you could spend thirty minutes each week studying investing, finance, and the tax laws and end up with the same $12,000.

Each time you decide to spend time or money on a venture, do this type of analysis to see what's most beneficial. If you could make twice that much on the house and the risk factor was the same, then it might be better to flip the house. But don't miss six months of Saturdays with your kids and find out later you were spinning your wheels.

I'm not at all dismissing the starting of a business, but I previously ran a small business and was astounded at how much work was involved. I think most people, as I did, underestimate how much work that can be. According to Dr. Stanley in *The Millionaire Next Door*, a very large portion of millionaires are business owners and entrepreneurs. This may well be your way to wealth, but make sure you know what you are getting into. Also consider that you won't retain as much of the income you do realize, as opposed to earning it in the stock market.

I don't want to beat a dead horse here, but most of us get paid for doing our jobs. Every day we show up at work, we must produce a service or product. Whatever I did the day before doesn't matter; I must produce it again and again to infinity. When I stop working, those checks stop rolling in.

When I built houses, I had to show up every day and replicate the process over and over to get paid. I'm not saying every day was always the same task, but each day involved a step in the house-building process. If I didn't show up, I didn't get paid. There was a finite number of houses I could build, and therefore a finite amount of money I could earn for my effort. If this effort stopped, so would my income source.

If I lined up ten houses, I would have ten times the work, and ten times the stress. I could build fewer houses and be more efficient, making more money off one house. But as the number went up, I would become less efficient and make less money per house.

You too have a finite amount of work that you can do in your life. There are a finite number of hours and a finite amount of times you can replicate a given task, whatever your job. As a general rule, when your workload increases, your efficiency decreases. As the amount of work I'm trying to accomplish goes up, my efficiency at any given task will generally go down as a general rule. If I build one house, I'm very efficient. If I build ten at the same time, I would have more scheduling, estimating, customers, employees, and suppliers. My world would become a lot more hectic. While I would probably increase my income, I wouldn't make ten times the money.

This is not the case with investing. If I own fifteen great stocks that I actively manage, it doesn't matter if I invest $1,000, $10,000, $100,000, or

$1,000,000; it's the same amount of work. If the amount I make this year increases by $1,000, $10,000, $100,000, or $1,000,000, my workload does not increase. Moving the decimal place doesn't cost me any more work. Whereas my job can only produce a finite amount of wealth for me, there's no limit to how much I can make investing because I don't have to keep replicating or increasing my effort.

I'm not saying I won't continue to do stock research, (because I will). My research time stays constant regardless of how much profit I make. In other words, the amount of money I have can increase to infinity, but my workload does not increase. It's no more work to manage $1,000,000 of stock if you keep the same number of stocks and increase the amount in each stock you own, versus managing $10,000. That's a rare concept in general, but especially in the world of money. Working for money is one of the least efficient ways to build wealth. You must work to obtain money in the first place, but if you earn from investments, you will get to keep a lot more of it.

In the earlier scenario, **Money Earned Working versus Money Earned Investing**, you have fifty percent *more* spendable income if you earn your money through investing rather than working for it. This is the reason so many rich people invest and often how they get rich and stay that way. If you want to be wealthy, you must learn how to play this game.

You must also realize that there is no political will to fix this. Not that I want it changed, as it's often the best chance for people like me to get ahead. However, many working-class people don't understand the tax code, nor do they try because it is so complex. Virtually all wealthy people in both political parties employ strategies to avoid taxes or reduce taxes. They can afford to hire accountants and lawyers to keep them from paying these taxes while they are "sticking up for the little guy" and railing against other politicians for "not paying their fair share." Meanwhile, when you get an extra job to help build yourself a retirement nest egg, you get taxed at your highest income bracket. So much for the little guy, right?

Again, I am not minimizing taking a job. After all, that's how I made enough money to save and initially invest in the stock market. That's also why I stress the importance of saving and investing at an early age. Eventually, what you can save becomes insignificant in comparison to the returns you make when money works for you.

As I mentioned earlier, I have known many people who work like crazy to get a promotion that bumps them from an income of $100,000 per year to $115,000 per year, yet they work many hours of weekly overtime just to earn that pay bump. Sometimes they do so at the expense of their family or their health. I don't have to trade any of those things when I make an extra $10,000 per year in the stock market. In fact, I can do it from any beach in the world with Internet access. I don't have to deal with a boss, customers, clients, or suppliers. I rarely need to speak with someone else to manage my portfolio. It's easier than working for the money and I get to keep more of it too.

In case you were wondering, this concept also works in reverse when you make monetary charitable donations. Did you know it is possible to gift stocks to charitable organizations? When you do, they get to keep more of your donation, and you get a bigger tax deduction. Talk about a win-win. Here's a basic example for you to follow:

Let's say you are still in that $110,000 income tax bracket, and your top marginal rate is still twenty-eight percent. If you worked at your part-time job to make the extra $10,000, you would be down to $6,710 after paying state and federal taxes. This is *before* paying any social security tax.

> $10,000 x .28 = $2,800 (federal taxes)
> $10,000 x .049 = $490 (New Mexico state tax)
> $2,800 + $490 = $3,290 (total taxes) $10,000- $3,290=
> $6,710 remaining to donate to a charity or church
>   of your choice.

After you donate the $6,710 to charity, you can deduct this amount from your taxes. Your tax bracket is still twenty-eight percent and your total tax deduction is $6,710.

Taxes

The basic math looks like this:

$6,710 x .28 = $1,878.80 (projected federal tax refund)
$6,710 x .049 = $328 (projected state tax refund)
Total return: $2,207.59

(Keep in mind social security taxes will not be refunded)

Takeaway: Your charity received $6,710 to help with their cause. You made $10,000 and gave it away. You receive a $2,207.59 tax refund. Yes, it really is that complicated and stupid. So what would happen if you donated the stocks directly to the charity or church of your choice?

$10,000 worth of stock X goes directly to your charity; they can sell stock X tax-free. They get the full $10,000 worth of benefit from your generosity. You get to deduct the entire $10,000 from your taxes.
$10,000 x .28 federal tax deduction = $2,800
$10,000 x .049 = $490 (New Mexico state income tax deduction; yours may differ)
$2,800 + $490= $3,249 total projected tax refund/credit
$10,000 - $3,290 = $6,710 (what it cost me)

My charity would enjoy the benefit of the entire $10,000 and my generosity only cost me $6,710. This again is *tax avoidance*, and it's perfectly legal. Why do you think so many wealthy folks set up charitable foundations? Aside from wanting to genuinely help others who are less fortunate, they get to enjoy the tax benefits. I certainly don't blame people for doing everything they legally can to avoid taxes—unless they try to raise everyone else's taxes to pay for their generosity.

For instance, I decided to donate two shares of Priceline to our church. I had paid $473.50 per share, so my total investment was $947. I held the stock for about six years; the stocks were worth $1,600 per share, which came out to a 238 percent return. I became a little concerned about the stock, so I decided to trim my holdings. I then donated the shares to my church. My church could then sell them for $3,200 total and keep all the money because they are tax exempt. I get to write off $3,200 as a charitable donation. At the end of the year, I will get back roughly one third in the form of a tax refund, which is about the same amount I initially invested.

In the end, I shared my financial blessings and gave my church $3,200. The government returned enough of my money withheld for taxes, which covered my initial investment. It's not unlike the Bible story at the beginning of the book in which the good servant doubled the talents he was given and then returned the money to his master. I try to be a good steward of what I have been given, and that's basically what money management is about—being a good steward.

Bottom Line: There are good and bad ways to give money and earn money. They are not all created equal. The better you become at knowing the differences, the more money you will have. Your tax situation will depend on many factors, including your marital status, your income, the state you live in, your number of dependents—to infinity. You can keep more of your money if you acquire it from investing rather than from working for it. The same goes for giving. You will have a lot more to give away if you do it in the most efficient manner possible.

8

PRIORITIZE AND
EDUCATE YOURSELF

IN MY OPINION, THE first step in the educational process is to decide that money is important. If you're unwilling to make sacrifices that support its significance, then you can close this book right now. However, if you:

1. **Don't want to be using plastic bread sacks to insulate your feet from the rain because you can't afford a good pair of boots;**
2. **Don't want to watch loved ones continue to struggle and be powerless to help them financially;**
3. **Want to help your children by paying for braces or college;**
4. **Don't want your family to struggle paying your funeral expenses;**

Then, money is important. Here and now, decide you want to improve the quality of your own life and those you care about. If you are waiting on the government to step in and help, you are wasting your time. If you have decided that it's crucial to have the means to support your family in a comfortable lifestyle for the rest of your lives, get started. Once you have made a priority list the rest is not complicated. It's not easy, but it's not complicated.

Ramsey says money management is eighty percent behavior, and I agree.

- Prioritize what is important.
- Educate yourself.
- Evaluate where you are now.
- Design a plan (Determine where you want to be and how to get there). Implement your plan.
- Evaluate your plan's effectiveness; if it's not working, change your plan, but not necessarily your goal.
- Recheck your list to make sure your priorities haven't changed; if they have, start over.

Prioritize Your Life

As you make a list of your priorities, be thoughtful and imaginative. Take your time and imagine what your life will be like in five, ten, and twenty-five years. What would you like for it to resemble? If you struggle with this, ask yourself what your parents or older friends and relatives do for fun. What are their regrets, passions, and interests? What do they find rewarding, and what do they wish that had wasted less time doing when they were younger? If they could go back in time, what would they change as far as preparing for the future? What has surprised them, and does their situation differ greatly from where they imagined themselves to be now? What's good and bad about their situation?

Be objective and use these answers as a thoughtful framework to plan your own future. You may find some common threads in your answers. Usually, I have noticed that people wish they had maintained better health and nurtured their relationships with family and friends. They also wish they had prepared better for their financial future. While some wish they had better jobs, I have yet to meet anyone who wishes they had spent more time working. Nor have I met anyone who was sorry they spent time with their family, or wished they had less money. These are just a few of the reasons why my priority list looks like it does. Your priority list certainly does not have to mirror mine, but you need one. It is like a good compass in a storm; when things get hectic, you know exactly where to focus your efforts.

Prioritize and Educate Yourself

Personal finance should be broken into three main categories:

1. Saving
2. Investing
3. Tax avoidance

You could argue that producing money to save in the first place is important, but I'm not trying to convince you to get the job with the most income-earning potential. Only you can make that decision. Again, this can all be summarized by where you place your priorities.

> ### *A priority list is like a good compass in a storm; when things get hectic, you know exactly where to focus your efforts.*

Bottom Line: Money is important. Prioritize your life; what is most important to you?

9

MY READING LIST

EDUCATION IS A LIFELONG endeavor. This includes learning about finances. There is always something new to learn and older skills and knowledge to polish. Please understand you can't do it once, and never do it again. It's much like starting an exercise routine—the beginning is generally the most difficult part. However, once you have the basic knowledge required, you will maintain your progress more easily.

I had a friend who would decide to start working out again every few weeks. He was a former high school jock who, like most of us, no longer looked like a jock. Every few weeks, he would psyche himself up to get back in shape. However, rather than starting out slowly and working his way into a routine, he would "max out" by lifting some ridiculously heavy weights. Naturally, he was proud of his accomplishment. This time would be a new beginning, or so he thought. The next day the soreness would set in, and he struggled to get out of bed. The following day, he would feel even worse. He would waste an entire week of feeling lousy before he felt up to working out again. And by then, his temporary, euphoric motivation was gone. He wouldn't touch another weight until weeks had passed because of his awful experience. The cycle would repeat itself once he talked himself into trying again.

I'm convinced that had he started out slowly, he would have experienced a better outcome. Instead, he viewed exercise as a whimsical fad, not a life-style change to commit to for the rest of his life. Because he desired to be instantly fit, he tried skipping the tedious part and failed time after time. Investing is much the same way. Educating yourself takes a while, and many tend to skip this step. They start investing right away without putting work into the difficult part of learning why and how to invest. Please don't be that guy, the one so anxious to get started that you run out and sink a ton of money into stocks you know nothing about. There is no reason to rush investing.

Managing money is a lifelong process. And it can be fun. I know that waiting seems boring, but don't jump in without first putting in the necessary work. Warren Buffet, arguably the best investor of all time, spends about eighty percent of his time reading. If you want to be good at this, commit the time to educating yourself.

Books to Transform Your Finances

1. *Total Money Makeover* by Dave Ramsey
2. *Idiot's Guide to Investing* by Edward T. Koch & Debra Johnson
3. *Beating the Street* by Peter Lynch
4. *One Up on Wall Street* by Peter Lynch
5. *Motley Fool Investment Guide* by David and Tom Gardner

My reading list is rather long, but I recommend starting with *Total Money Makeover*, even if you're clear of debt and tend to be good with money. I used that same rationale to justify why I didn't need to read the book. I have always been good with money. While I never had much of it, I simply did without rather than purchasing things I couldn't afford. I was never late paying bills because I rarely borrowed money. In fact, when I finally read *Total Money Makeover* for the first time, I owed a small amount of money on my truck and my house. I had a few hundred thousand dollars in land, retirement accounts, and other assets. I was doing pretty well by most people's standards.

The Money Talk

What I gleaned most from the book was learning about a "rich" person's thought process. I learned how to make a long-term budget that would last my lifetime. This wasn't some short-term euphoric fad like my buddy's work-out program. It didn't require personal motivation to try again every few weeks; it was a system that prompted a lifestyle change. After implementing this new system, my wife and I paid off our first home.

Lindsey and I worked like crazy for two and a half years, "living like no one else, so later we could live like no one else." I paid the mortgage and household expenses from my check, and Lindsey applied her check to childcare; the leftover amount was allocated toward the principal on our mortgage. We had already eliminated all our other debt, and this was the last piece of the puzzle. I kept a ledger, and each time we got paid, I paid the bank. Each month we saw the balance shrink on our mortgage. I knew it was a quick payoff on our mortgage; still, it was like watching water getting ready to boil—agonizingly slow month after month. Within about two and a half years, the balance was low enough that I sold a few shares of stock to finish paying off the house.

We took a family trip to the bank in September 2013 to take possession of our home. That was a proud day for us. We were completely debt-free, and that changed our lives. Ramsey was correct; the pillows really did feel softer at night. I had a great sense of security just knowing that no matter what, my family and I had somewhere to live.

A few days later, Lindsey and I were both temporarily laid off from our jobs. We didn't know how long the layoff would last, or when we would collect another paycheck. Further, our daughter was born soon after on October 5. Within one month of paying off our house, we were laid off and we had a new baby. Talk about God's good timing. Some might believe it was a coincidence, but we knew the layoff was not a big deal. With a mortgage payment and no income or emergency fund, it would have been. A joyful blessing could easily have been overshadowed by fear.

Instead, we rode out the layoffs with little to no impact on our short-term or long-term finances. Again, Ramsey was right. It rained and we were wearing our raincoats. We saw a lot of our coworkers worry about the layoffs. Meanwhile, we could hang out with our newborn and enjoy every minute with our growing family.

After reading *Total Money Makeover*, I soon began sharing Ramsey's contempt for debt. At first, I thought he was a bit paranoid. After all, I had been taught my entire life that debt was a necessity if you ever hoped to have anything. Maybe conventional wisdom also taught you that debt was a tool for leverage, and it was okay to use it. As I've grown older, I have seen the wisdom of his words. Now I know what debt really is: a crushing burden that adds risk and uncertainty to life.

Ramsey advocates paying off your house. I always struggled with that notion because my logic went like this:

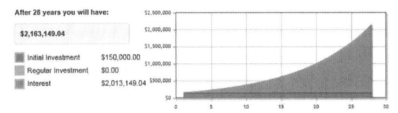

I owed $150,000 on my house, and I had amassed enough money in investments to pay off my mortgage. However, I reasoned that in twenty-eight years, (with a thirty-year mortgage) by using the *Rule of 72*, with a ten percent average return from the market, that $150,000 would double every seven years. The first turnover at seven years would be $300,000, the second in fourteen years would be $600,000; at twenty-one years, it would compound to $1.2 million. In twenty-eight years, it would turn in to about $2.2 million.

If I let it go the full thirty years, it would turn into $2.6 million.

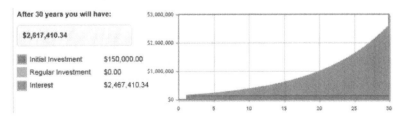

The Money Talk

That being the case, why would I remove $150,000 from the stock market to pay off a house that *might* be worth $300,000 in that same timeframe? On the surface, that math made sense to me, and I was convinced I was right.

Yet I was leaving out one very important variable: risk. As Mr. Ramsey says, it will rain, so you better have a raincoat. In other words, bad things will happen, so you need to have an emergency fund and a plan in place. People will get sick, get divorced, have ill relatives, and other life-altering events. These will occur over the next thirty years while you are busy paying off your house. Having your home paid off is invaluable when something bad does happen. It is a tremendous relief to not worry about how you'll pay your mortgage note when the pay cut, job loss, or illness strikes.

I'm stubborn, and wasn't quite convinced this alone was reason enough to forfeit that much potential income. So, I discussed it with a friend of mine named Jimmy Carrell. I outlined my basic logic, and then he asked me a question I had not considered. First, "How much are your monthly payments?" They were $1,212. Second, "If you put your payment money in an index mutual fund, rather than paying the bank every month, what would it be in the same timeframe?"

Admittedly, I had not considered that scenario. I looked up an online investment calculator and plugged in the numbers. Depositing $1,212 every month into an index mutual fund for twenty-eight years with a ten percent rate of return would amount to roughly $2.1 million.

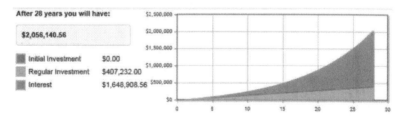

Doing this for the entire thirty years would result in $2.5 million.

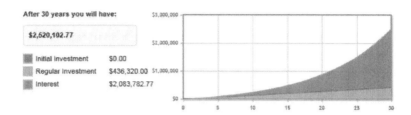

After 30 years you will have:

$2,520,102.77

Initial Investment	$0.00
Regular Investment	$436,320.00
Interest	$2,083,782.77

Scenario #1

Pay the mortgage note every month ($1,212), and leave $150,000 in a mutual fund, returning ten percent for thirty years = $2,617,410

Scenario #2

Sell enough stock to pay off the house ($150,000); continue putting the mortgage note ($1,212) into the stock market for thirty years with a ten percent rate of return = $2,520,102.

The result of leaving the money in the stock market, or paying off the house and investing the payments for thirty years afterward would be nearly the same. The main difference between each scenario was that if I paid off my house, I would eliminate a huge amount of uncertainty and risk. I, like most people, discounted risk as having no monetary value. This is foolish.

Here's an example of varying risk factors: if you invest money in government bonds, you receive a low yield, one to two percent return, because they are guaranteed by the government. If you invest money into high-quality bonds, you make a little more money, but you also assume a bit more risk. If you buy junk bonds, you earn even more interest because the company may not have stellar credit or they are in danger of going broke. The greater the quick return, the greater the risk. If you bet on craps and win, you receive a huge return immediately because the odds are great that you will lose all your money. I believe you should be rewarded or punished according to the amount of risk you take. When I was initially doing my figuring, I completely ignored that. Live and learn, they say. Ramsey dispels several debt myths in this book. Many of these myths are touted as conventional wisdom. One such myth is how you save money by not paying off your home because you can deduct mortgage interest on your taxes. If someone tells you this, they cannot do math.

> *This situation is one more opportunity to discover if your CPA can add. If you do not have a $10,000 tax deduction and you are in a 30% bracket, you will have to pay $3,000 in taxes on that $10,000. According to the myth, we should send $10,000 in interest to the bank so we don't have to send $3,000 in taxes to the IRS. Personally, I think I will live debt-free and not make a $10,000 trade for $3,000. However, any of you who want $3,000 of your taxes paid, just e-mail me and I will personally pay $3,000 of your taxes as soon as your check for $10,000 clears into my bank account. I can add.* [28]

—Dave Ramsey,
Total Money Makeover

This and other principles are outlined in Ramsey's book. He explains what to do, why it's a good idea, and how to do it. It is a basic blueprint for someone to get—and stay—debt free. It's very important to understand this principle. Through the years, I've seen people go broke over and over because of debt. It is still possible to lose everything, even without debt, if you suffer from an addiction. That generally happens when one borrows money against an owned property to lose an owned home. If you don't borrow money from anyone for any reason, you obey the law, and have health and liability insurance, you really don't have to worry about losing everything you own. While it's possible, it's not very likely.

Ramsey also advocates setting up a long-term plan to stay out of debt by budgeting and planning. Many people don't understand that budgeting is nothing more than spending money deliberately. If you let money tend to itself, it will disappear. If you buy a Starbucks coffee every day for $5, you'll spend $1,825 per year. If it's in your budget, there is nothing wrong with that. If at the end of the year your friends tell you they are going on a cruise and it costs $1,825 and you think, "Man, if I had just saved my money rather than buying all that Starbucks coffee, I could afford to go on that cruise." then you did not spend your money deliberately and therefore budgeted poorly.

If, on the other hand you think, "That Starbucks coffee every morning made my year and not going on that cruise was a small sacrifice to guarantee getting my Starbucks." then you did spend deliberately and you budgeted correctly.

Budgeting is not all doing without, like most people seem to think. Budgeting is about making conscious decisions with your money, and then making that money do what you want. Maintaining an emergency fund is another great reason to budget your money. You should not put any money in the stock market unless you can leave it untouched for at least five years. If you don't have an emergency fund, wait to put money in the stock market until you do. Because the market fluctuates drastically at times, you need to be positioned to wait it out. People often put money in the stock market, and then the stock drops or the market tanks. This is fairly normal. If you can wait it out though, it's not a big deal. In fact, it could very well be a great time to add to your portfolio. However, if an emergency pops up and leaves you needing to sell at a huge loss because you need the money right away, you might swear off the market for life and blame everyone and their brother for the loss, even though it was all a lack of preparation on your part.

While *Total Money Makeover* is more about getting out of debt and setting up a long-term plan to stay that way, it doesn't really address investing. This topic is where Ramsey and I have conflicting opinions. Before filing for bankruptcy, Ramsey built his wealth by selling real estate. As a result, his philosophy differs because his experience diverges from mine. I've heard him say that he puts his money into mutual funds and eventually rolls that in to real estate. He advocates using mutual funds for investment purposes and steering clear of individual stocks. I don't know Ramsey personally, but he is often criticized for his investment advice. It's not that he is wrong; if you don't have any interest in learning how to manage stocks, going the mutual fund route is sound advice. If you went no further than becoming debt-free and putting your savings into index mutual funds, you would still retire very wealthy.

However, I believe you can get better returns with individual stocks. Why would we want to manage stocks if an index mutual fund has historically made around ten percent? One good reason is because you enjoy doing it; another is you might be able to do a few percentage points better. Does one or two percentage points really matter after all? Absolutely. Let's look at the difference a couple percentage points can make.

The first example is ten percent return over the course of a forty-year span from age twenty-five to sixty-five. We will look at a $100 investment with nothing else added for the entire time.

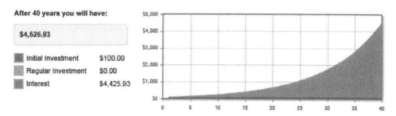

Impressive, right? A one-time investment will increase from $100 to $4,526.29 over a forty-year period. But at a twelve percent rate of return, it would be $9,305.03.

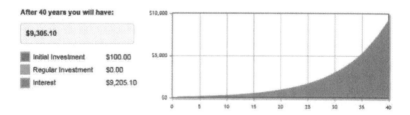

A two-percent increase more than *doubles* your earnings. Without a doubt, that small increase makes a tremendous difference in your return over a long period of time, and it's all due to compounding interest.

Bottom Line: There is a better way to invest. From my experience, managing your own money through individual stocks will yield better returns than mutual funds. If you have the desire to learn how to invest and make your money work for you, there is a better way. Regardless, *do not* put money into investments until you have a "raincoat" (***emergency fund***).

10

WHAT IS INVESTING?

WHAT A SILLY QUESTION. Everyone knows what investing is, right? Well, no, many people don't, because their behavior and speech indicate otherwise. What does investing mean to you?

> *Investment: to invest is to allocate money (or sometimes another resource, such as time) in the expectation of some benefit in the future. This article concerns the use of the term in finance. In finance, the expected future benefit from investment is a return. The return may consist of capital gain and/or investment income, including dividends, interest, rental income etc.*
>
> —Wikipedia

Warren Buffett states:

> *Investing is often described as the process of laying out money now in the expectation of receiving more money in the future. At Berkshire we take a more demanding approach, defining investing as the transfer to others of purchasing power now with the reasoned expectation of receiving more purchasing power – after taxes have been paid on nominal gains – in the future. More succinctly, investing is forgoing consumption now to have the ability to consume*

more at a later date. From our definition there flows an important corollary: The riskiness of an investment is not measured by beta (a Wall Street term encompassing volatility and often used in measuring risk) but rather by the probability – the reasoned probability – of that investment causing its owner a loss of purchasing-power over his contemplated holding period. Assets can fluctuate greatly in price and not be risky as long as they are reasonably certain to deliver increased purchasing power over their holding period.

These two definitions seem to mirror each other, but they are quite different. In the Wikipedia definition, one receives a benefit in the future, such as a "return." That, according to most people, means you are going to have a greater amount of money later. According to Mr. Buffett, one gives up purchasing power now with the expectation of increased purchasing power later, after paying taxes. I like Mr. Buffett's definition better. For example, I hear a lot about investing in *Certificates of Deposit (CDs)* at present rates of 1.5 percent. In my opinion, that is not an investment. Inflation is historically three percent. If you earn less than that, you are *losing* purchasing power, not gaining it. Even if the amount of money you have increases, you are still losing purchasing power.

Here's an example:

Candy bars cost $1, and you have $10. You can buy ten candy bars. If you put your $10 into a **CD** earning 1.5 percent, using the Rule of 72, (72 divided by 1.5 percent) in just forty-eight short years would have $20. I cannot see the future, but I'll bet a large sum that $20 will not buy ten candy bars in forty-eight years. The amount of money I have increases, but my purchasing power does not. I may not be able to buy a pack of gum in forty-eight years with that $20, but on paper it says I made a profit. To add insult to injury, I now owe taxes on said profit.

Many people believe putting money into a house counts as investing. If someone can buy a house at a very low price, then sell it at a price greater than three percent compounded return (the historical rate of inflation), then they made a profit. For ease of math we will ignore taxes and closing costs.

The Money Talk

If I buy a house this year for $100,000 and I sell it next year for $103,000, did I make a profit? If inflation is climbing at three percent, $100,000 x .03 (three percent) = $103,000 I'm at a break-even point. If I sell the house for more, I made a profit; if I sell it for less, I have not. This could count as investing. Some do this with much success, but most people cannot.

Have I increased my purchasing power? If I sell the house for more than $103,000, plus taxes and fees, then I've made a profit. Of course, we must factor in the risk and work involved. If you buy the house to live in, that is one thing, but if you are "investing," these factors must be considered, along with the opportunity cost of having your money tied up.

I'm not implying you don't need a house; Peter Lynch says home ownership is more important than investing.[29] It's important to own a place to live, but it often does not outpace inflation. If your house increases in value at a rate lower than inflation, it is a house and not an investment. There is nothing wrong with that, but it does not increase your purchasing power. Also, consider that most mortgages are paid back at a rate of interest greater (six percent) than the historic rate of inflation (three percent). Thus, you'll end up paying *twice* the amount you borrowed with a thirty-year mortgage, even with today's low interest rates. Most of us will need a place to stay for the rest of our lives after we pay the house off; we typically can't sell it and harvest that gain anyway. Some might downsize and keep the difference in profit, but that doesn't make one wealthy.

However, if you pay off your home, then use your mortgage payment to invest, you will be well on your way to becoming wealthy. If you buy a home that costs $150,000 and spend $300,000 on it over a thirty-year period, you can sell it for $300,000 and have a zero increase in dollars "invested." You have simply saved $300,000. Additionally, you likely didn't increase purchasing power.

Don't get lost in the numbers. This information is to prove the importance of paying off a home. It is a huge accomplishment and something everyone should strive to do. Yet, it's only part of the big picture. You then need to invest the money you previously set aside for mortgage payments. Choose an investment that will outpace inflation (hopefully by quite a lot). Free up that mortgage payment by either paying cash for the home or getting a fifteen-year mortgage and paying it down as quickly as possible.

The Complete Idiot's Guide to Investing is another helpful book. While it has been years since I read this book for the first time, I am still influenced by its invaluable lessons. When I was younger, I lacked any family members or friends with meaningful knowledge of investing or the stock market. So when I first started reading about investing basics, I didn't even understand the terminology well enough to follow the articles. When a write-up mentioned **EBIDTA, Forward P/E, Generally Accepted Accounting Principles (GAAP)**, or **Trailing P/E** I had to shift gears and look up acronyms or accounting terms. This was back in the early '90s, before the Internet and smart phones. So, by the time I uncovered answers, I felt frustrated and stupid. Reading *The Complete Idiot's Guide to Investing* will help you build enough base knowledge to follow a conversation or article. While it may go more in depth than necessary, you'll learn a lot of the common terms used in investing. It will also help you do some meaningful research of your own.

I also recommend reading Peter Lynch's books, *One Up on Wall Street* and *Beating the Street*. Lynch is one of the best money managers the world has ever known. He managed the Magellan Fund at Fidelity Investments between 1977 and 1990, in which he averaged a 29.2 percent annual return. He consistently more than doubled the S&P 500 market index, making it the best performing mutual fund in the world. Under his tenure, assets under management increased from $18 million to $14 billion.

Mr. Lynch has the unique ability to put his insight into layman's terms so that even I can understand them. I have pages and pages of his quotes, along with those of Warren Buffet, on my desktop. I print out a few for quick reference so I can browse over them in my idle time. These words often reveal a lot about these men's insight and philosophy. They offer perspective. I liken their insight to Solomon's fabled magic ring that kept him from becoming too happy when things were good, or too sad when things were bad. The ring's inscription read, "This too shall pass."

The Money Talk

In 2016, I read this excerpt from an interview with Lynch.

Well, 1990 was a situation where I think it's almost exactly six years ago approximately now. In the summer of 1990, the market's around 3000. Economy's doing okay. And Saddam Hussein decides to walk in and invade Kuwait. So we have invasion of Kuwait and President Bush sends 500,000 troops to Saudi to protect Saudi Arabia. There's a very big concern about, you know, "Are we going to have another Vietnam War?" A lot of serious military people said, "This is going to be a terrible war." Iraq has the fourth largest army in the world. They really fought very well against Iran. These people are tough. This is going to be a long, awful thing.

So, people were very concerned about that, but, in addition, we had a very major banking crisis. All the major New York City banks, Bank of America, the real cornerstone of this country, were really in trouble. And this is a lot different than if W. T. Grant went under or Penn Central went under. Banking is really tight. And you had to hope that the banking system would hold together and that the Federal Reserve understood that Citicorp, Chase, Chemical, Manufacturers Hanover, Bank of America were very important to this country and that they would survive.

And then we had a recession. Unlike '87, you called companies, in 1990 you called companies and say, "Gee, our business is startin' to slip. Inventories are startin' to pile up. We're not doing that well." So, you really at that point in time had to belief the whole thing would hold together, that we wouldn't have a major war. You really had to have faith in the future of this country in 1990. In '87, the fundamentals were terrific and it was—it was like one of those three for two sales at the K-Mart. Things were marked down. It was the same story.

Or this one from the same interview:

What is Investing?

1982 was a very scary period for this country. We've had nine recessions since World War II. This was the worst. Fourteen-percent inflation. We had a twenty percent prime rate, fifteen percent long governments. It was ugly. And the economy was really much in a free-fall and people were really worried, "Is this it? Has the American economy had it? Are we going to be able to control inflation?" I mean there were a lot of very uncertain times. You had to say to yourself, "I believe it is. I believe in stocks. I believe in companies. I believe they can control this. And this is an anomaly. Double-digit inflation is rare thing. Doesn't happen very often." And, in fact, one of my shareholders wrote me and said, "Do you realize that over half the companies in your portfolio are losing money right now?" I looked up, he was right, or she was right. But I was ready. I mean I said, "These companies are going to do well once the economy comes back. We've got out of every other recession. I don't see why we won't come out of this one." And it came out and once we came back, the market went north.

I lived through both time periods, and I still remember the flood of bad news coming from the media outlets. This time was different from all the other times; this time we were really, really, really going broke. We would be out hunting and fishing just to survive. Civilization as we knew it was going to collapse. As of 2016, we were still in Iraq and fighting in Afghanistan (wars and military conflicts will be ongoing). There was another banking crisis in 2008, which required a government bailout to prevent the majority from declaring bankruptcy. It seems some industry is always on the brink of collapse. These excerpts are used to draw parallels between events of the past and our current reality.

Bottom Line: Turmoil is constant; if you wait for the market to "stabilize" or for things to "settle down," you will wait indefinitely and the time to invest will never come.

11

PERSPECTIVE:
SURVIVING THE COMING COLLAPSE

INCIDENTALLY "Y2K" WAS MORE of the same. Everyone rushed out and stocked up on food and generators, stockpiling ammunition, and preparing for the end of civilization, as we knew it. Y2K, you'll remember, was a glitch in computer programming. Prior to the turn of the millennium, it appeared that as clocks rolled over from 1999 to 2000, all computer systems would crash. The ensuing failure would cause a complete shutdown of the entire world. We were told it would cripple the farming, shipping, and food transportation industries. There would be pandemonium and people eating each other to keep from starving. Okay, that last notion might be exaggerating, but you get the idea.

Guess what happened on January 1, 2000 at 12:00 a.m.? Nothing. Almost no computers crashed, no shipping went down, and there were no widespread blackouts. The U.S. economy kept ticking away, and everyone woke up and went on with life as usual.

As a child in the 1970s, I recall the media trying to convince us we were moving into another Ice Age. The temperature would drop and the earth would cool. We would all starve because the farming harvests would be miniscule and unable to produce enough food. We constantly lived in fear that then-superpower, the Soviet Union (Russia), was going to declare war on the United States. It was imminent and we were all going to die. If the initial nuclear blast did not kill you, then you would surely die from radiation poisoning. Or, if you survived both of those scenarios, you would certainly starve to death from the nuclear winters. The sun would be blotted out for years, crops would fail, and all life on earth would cease to exist. How's that for an uplifting childhood?

Soon after, we began experiencing "global warming" and the fear of another Ice Age was over. Man had now ruined earth; our aerosol deodorant spray had eaten holes in the ozone and we would all fry. The deforestation of the Amazon rainforest had accelerated the process, and we were all going to cook under the sun's intensive heat. This heat would be so powerful that polar ice caps would melt, and sea levels would rise, thus flooding the whole world. Again, we'd starve because there would be no arable land to farm food. All the fresh water would be used up, so we might've even died of thirst before we had a chance to starve or die of skin cancer.

Then the world became ripe for a pandemic virus, as evidenced by Hollywood and their numerous movies made about these inevitable disasters, including *Water World*, *The Stand*, *The Road*, *An Inconvenient Truth*, and *Outbreak*. It was all over the news; Ebola was going to wipe us out. A friend even called to warn me about the "Eboli" virus. I assumed it was a cross between Ebola and E-coli bacteria, making it double dangerous and ten times as deadly. It would soon sweep across the entire country and kill us all!

Perhaps you're beginning to see how the media business has reported one depressing story after another for my entire life. It seems the media feast on exaggerating the next dire prediction of over-population, economic collapse, and earth wiped clean of all life forms.

As each of these horrible events were about to occur, I didn't have enough money to worry about what would happen to it. I was only concerned with keeping my family and myself alive through the impending disasters. As I got older and began reading Lynch's books, I realized these impending-doom scenarios were nothing new. This had been going on for the duration of Lynch's life and even much longer. I concluded this was overblown fear mongering.

Now, eventually something bad will happen. I don't blame anyone for storing food and supplies in case of disaster. In fact, I think we all should, just as we store candles and generators for power outages. Preparing for such catastrophes is much like taking out a life insurance policy. You hope you don't need it anytime soon, but it never hurts to be prepared.

With all that said, remember that humans are adaptable. The next time warnings of an economic collapse, meteors, flooding, droughts, elections, viruses, or food and water shortages come along, don't sell everything you own and head for the hills. It will likely be okay in the long run. As I get older, I realize that in the event of a complete economic meltdown and governmental collapse, money would be worthless. Those who are too scared to invest imagine that having their money in cash will ensure their security. Cash is great, but it is a poor investment unless there is *deflation*. But when Ben Bernanke, the former Federal Bank Chairman, openly stated that he would "throw money out of helicopters" rather than have deflation, you can be fairly sure that deflation won't happen.

Money is paper; you could probably burn it if necessary or use it for pillow stuffing. But it has no intrinsic value. You can't eat it, smoke it, or drink it. The only reason it has value is because people have faith it is an accepted form of payment for something they desire. If that faith disappears, so does the "value" attached to money. Historically, when a government collapses, their paper currency becomes worthless. If you approach money in this context, you realize investing doesn't hold as much risk as you originally thought. If the market pulls back, I assure you there will be stories all over the news predicting a "blood bath" or "blood in the streets" or some other event. However, if you watch individual stocks, you will notice a lot of great deals. People will flee the market in panic, selling out at the worst possible time before they "lose any more money." This presents an enormous opportunity for anyone who keeps a level head and has the right perspective.

Whenever I become anxious about what's going in our country, the world, politics, or the economy, I like to read Ecclesiastes ("There is nothing new under the sun.") and quotes from Lynch and Buffet. If you follow these authors, you will discover that simply changing the names of countries, companies, and dates make their writings relevant to anything current in world affairs.

You will also find these authors are masters of perspective. Look at the news in the same context. You will soon realize it's the same old stuff being circulated. Just a few names change. If you watch the news tonight, there will be some dramatic music, one or two tragic stories of some horrible mishaps, a tsunami, a fire, an explosion, or terrorist attack. The reporters will touch on politics and the economy. They will conclude with a story of the next possible disaster, and promise to keep you informed of any further developments. It's hard not to worry when you're surrounded by these stories on Facebook, Twitter, and Yahoo news. But if you look at everything in context, (or ignore most of this doomsday talk) you can really prosper, and even profit.

If you realize there is no real way to protect yourself from a nuclear war or the earth warming or cooling, and instead work at building real wealth, you will prosper. If the government collapses, paper money in a buried mason jar is useless. However, owning stock in a thriving company can afford you trips all over the world, a second home, college tuition for your kids, or large sums of cash to give to your favorite church, cause, or charity.

My favorite Warren Buffet quotes include the following:

> *Over the long term, the stock market news will be good. In the 20th century, the United States endured two world wars and other traumatic and expensive military conflicts, the Depression, a dozen or so recessions and financial panics, oil shocks, a fly epidemic, and the resignation of a disgraced president. Yet the Dow rose from 66 to 11,497 points.*

> *The line separating investment and speculation, which is never bright and clear, becomes blurred still further when most market*

*participants have recently enjoyed triumphs. Nothing sedates ratio-
nality like large doses of effortless money. After a heady experience
of that kind, normally sensible people drift into behavior akin to
that of Cinderella at the ball. They know that overstaying the fes-
tivities—that is, continuing to speculate in companies that have
gigantic valuations relative to the cash they are likely to generate
in the future—will eventually bring on pumpkins and mice. But
they nevertheless hate to miss a single minute of what is one helluva
party. Therefore, the giddy participants all plan to leave just seconds
before midnight. There's a problem, though: They are dancing in a
room in which the clocks have no hands.*

*Time is the friend of the wonderful business. It's the enemy of the
lousy business. If you're in a lousy business for a long time, you're
going to get a lousy result, even if you buy it cheap. If you're in
a wonderful business for a long time, even if you pay a little too
much going in, you're going to get a wonderful result if you stay in
a long time. The very term "value investing" is redundant. What
is investing if it is not the act of seeking value at least sufficient
to justify the amount paid? Consciously paying more for a stock
than its calculated value—in the hope that it can soon be sold for
a still-higher price—should be labeled speculation (which is neither illegal, immoral nor—in our view—financially fattening). We
select our marketable equity securities in much the way we would
evaluate a business for acquisition in its entirety.*

*We want businesses to be one (a) that we can understand; (b) with
favorable long-term prospects; (c) operated by honest and competent people; and (d) available at a very attractive price.*

Notice how well he puts things into realistic perspective?
In full disclosure, I don't agree with Buffett on everything. For instance,

he does not advise people to buy individual stock, but to stick with index mutual funds; he does, however, buy them himself. Based on most people's behavior, that is very sound advice. However, if you are willing to do the research and you are disciplined, I believe you can outperform mutual funds by investing in individual stocks. I don't know Buffett personally, but I'll guess he advocates mutual fund investment for the masses because most people want to buy stocks without doing enough research. If you don't want to do the necessary research, then he is absolutely right.

Fear and greed are our two biggest enemies. They both make people act irrationally. Fear will make you sell in a panic whenever there is a market pull back and you should instead be buying.

Greed will make you hang on when you know the fundamentals are falling apart and you should be selling or buying a pathetic long shot for a possible huge return you probably won't get, you want the middle ground. You want to calmly and rationally look at a situation and see it for what it is. It is either an opportunity or a place of danger. Distinguishing one from the other is usually obvious if we can divorce ourselves from emotion and make a logical, rational decision based on facts rather than feelings. I hear people tell me all the time that they have a "gut feeling." While this may work in some situations, it isn't the greatest approach with money. When I'm dealing with money, the only thing my gut tells me is that I am hungry. That's it.

When buying pathetic ***penny stocks***, many amateurs try for a grand slam. What's wrong with a base hit? If you can get on base eight out of ten times at bat, you can win almost every game you play. However, if you strike out most of the time you are up to bat, are you any better off? I would say no. Everyone wants to see the ball go over the fence, but my only concern is winning. If you do enough research and buy good companies, you can still hit some home runs. If you buy crappy long shots, you are going to lose the majority of your games. Buying the base hits is investing; buying the long shot is speculating. The investors almost always beat the speculators in the long run. When investing in mutual funds, you need to buy and forget it; don't try to move in and out. Buy them and hang on to them.

Investing in individual stocks is an entirely different ball game. You need to research and then buy. You need to continue researching after your purchase, monitoring the situation. You need to buy and do almost nothing. One of the hardest things, according to Lynch, is to ignore the bad news long enough to make money.

Lines Never Converge

Some people say stocks are risky, so here are a few of your general investment options. As you can see, stocks have handily beaten most of your "options" for over 150 years. Stocks have beaten gold and cash for over 200 years.

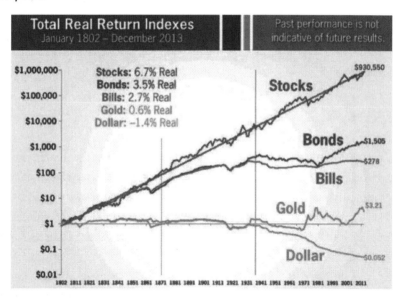

The next big meltdown may be the "big 'un," as Fred Sanford used to say, but if history is any indicator, it's probably not. The precipitous drop in 1929, the **Great Depression**, is a blip on the radar screen in the grand scheme of things. You can see the line signifying cash or bonds also diverges from that of stocks and never comes close again after a few years. While you may have some drops in your portfolio, remember that the amount should have

96

doubled in seven years. Even if your investments drop close to fifty percent, you are still at about the same place you would have been if you left it in CDs at today's near zero percent return. Around this time, the two lines should diverge and never come close to each other again. You will be forever ahead owning stocks rather than CDs.

Your money is a lot like wine in this instance. Have you ever saved up a really nice bottle of wine for a special occasion, only to find that you waited too long to enjoy it? All the delightful sweetness is gone, and that first sip tastes like vinegar. Your efforts to guard the wine in the long-term actually cost you the entire bottle. While the investments keep growing from now on getting bigger and bigger.

You can see from the graph below that **bonds, T-bills,** and the like do not have as many wild gyrations as stocks. But you can see they don't perform as well either. If you put $1,000 in a CD that returns three percent, it would reach $1,230 before taxes in just seven short years.

The same $1,000 would become $1,949 if left in stocks over the same period. While it could drop enough to get down to $1,230, it's highly unlikely. If you kept your money safely in cash, it would be worth a lot less than when you started due to inflation.

The "safe investment" would guarantee a loss, while the "risky" investment would not guarantee a profit. It would be all but guaranteed based on the market's past performance. The lines in performance will diverge and they will likely never come close again after seven years or so. The "risky" investments (stocks) will all but guarantee a gain and the "safe" investment (cash) will all but guarantee a loss.

There is a risk that is seldom discussed: *being too conservative with your investments*. Yes, your stocks may rise and fall precipitously. But most other investments would never reach that level in the first place. In this instance, safety is an illusion. You will have far less money if it's in a safe, but it doesn't go up and down either. That almost guarantees a lower return over the long haul.

Have you ever watched a child playing in the sand on a beach? Very young children like building sand castles. When they begin, they attempt to pick up the dry sand, which invariably runs through the cracks in their fingers. They look a bit confused, and then pick up more sand. Once more, it runs between their fingers, and soon they have lost all their sand.

This is what inflation will eventually do to your savings. You try to keep it in your hands because it is secure, but it eventually slips away. The child will eventually realize he can't hold on to the sand, so he will grab a pail and shovel if available. The shovel helps him pick up the sand, and he can quickly fill the bucket. The bucket lets the child transport the sand and soon he is molding a castle. If he figures out to use the wet sand, the process flies, and he can start really building a sand castle.

People who are fearful of investing are like the children still trying to acquire sand with their hands. They fail to realize that without a better sand retrieval system, they are unable to accumulate a sizable amount. The shovel and bucket are the equivalent of investment vehicles. They help you amass greater amounts in one area, transporting it to a place where the next wave won't wipe out your sand castle. Your portfolio is your sand castle; it must be protected from waves and mean little kids who want to stomp on it. The waves and mean kids are taxes, inflation, and "get-rich-quick" schemes.

Fear can be contagious; don't catch it.

Those still holding sand in their hands will warn you about the quantity you'll spill by using the shovel and bucket method. They will also warn you about the danger of tripping while you carry the bucket—you can potentially lose a lot of sand or drop the bucket altogether and then must refill it. This is like a **market correction**. Regardless, they will still explain away the dangers of your actions when you upgrade to a wheelbarrow and a scoop, or a backhoe and a dump truck. Yet, all they will have is a pitiful pile of sand slipping through their fingers. When you will spill more eventually as you drop a bucket, it will be an insignificant matter.

While I'm not berating these types of people nor belittling their struggles, I am urging you to steer away from their advice. Fear can be contagious;

don't catch it. Don't be paralyzed into doing nothing because you are scared to do the wrong thing.

Buffet has been investing long enough that no matter what arises, he has experienced it. If it is a war, panic about a banking collapse, or a thirty percent drop in the market, he has seen it and lived to tell about it. That reassurance makes it easier for me to search through the rubble and pick out great stock deals.

I highly recommend reading David and Tom Gardner's *The Motley Fool Investment Guide* as well. Fellow Lynch fans, the Gardner brothers operate a stock-advisory service and have an uncanny knack for picking great stocks. Their book builds on Lynch's foundation, and they further explain how you build wealth slowly over a handful of decades. They even say you can potentially "partner" with companies for the rest of your life by investing in their stock. They also detail what they look for in accounting fundamentals, which are useful for dissecting a company balance sheet. Their monthly newsletter, *Motley Fool Stock Advisor*, includes helpful investing information. They offer such a valuable service that I have more than paid for the yearly fee for my lifetime based on profit I've made by acting on their advice.

By now, I hope you see that investing is not just putting money somewhere and expecting a larger sum later. Rather, it's about obtaining a sufficient rate of return to increase the buying power that you had when you started investing. That means getting a return large enough to outpace inflation—hopefully by a wide margin.

Do you know anyone whose dream involves buying a couple of lakeside acres to build on after retirement? While they look at it as an investment, you need to understand something about this mentality. If at age thirty-five, you purchase a $50,000 lot to build your dream home in retirement, and you plan to retire at sixty-five, how much would the lot have to increase in value before it outperformed the same $50,000 invested in the stock market during those thirty years? It would have to be valued at nearly $900,000 before you surpassed what it would do in the stock market. While that isn't impossible, it is highly unlikely.

Let's look at a different scenario.

What if you invested $50,000 in the stock market for thirty years? By then the price of the lot would likely increase, but even if you had to purchase the lot for $200,000, you would still have $700,000 leftover for building your dream house. I like those numbers a lot better.

Something else I've seen on occasion is when someone buys that lot, it is secluded and private; however, after a few years other houses completely surround that lot and it's not the place the owners had envisioned at all. People come up with various schemes to make a quick buck on some type of venture, only to realize later it would have been more profitable and a lot less trouble to invest it in the market. The stock market has consistently outperformed any industry I know of over the long haul. Whenever you are tempted, do a careful analysis to ensure you will not suffer a lost opportunity somewhere else.

Bottom Line: Don't let the gloom-and-doom scenarios prevent you from preparing for your future. Don't let an imagined fear keep you from investing; this will bring about very real suffering. Whatever you choose to invest in, ensure you are getting the best possible return from your money.

12

DIFFERENT WAYS OF INVESTING

IF YOU DECIDE TO take the index mutual fund route, there are a few things you must know. The best way to buy mutual funds is to ***dollar cost average***. Create a regular schedule and invest a regular amount each time. It doesn't matter if the market is up or down. This is as easy as investing gets. You also don't need to pay a brokerage fee to buy index mutual funds; you can buy them directly and skip brokerage fees.

Buy $100 per week or month (whatever you can afford), and do it every time, regardless of the market's performance. Buy fewer shares when the market is high, and more shares when the market is lower. While that makes sense, the math is a little more convincing.

Let's say you are buying mutual fund X and the market is moving up and down, not really staying in one place. Let's say each month you save $100 to invest. The first month you invest and the mutual fund costs $20 per share and you buy five shares. The next month your index mutual fund jumps to $25 per share and you can only buy four shares. The next month the bottom falls out and it's back down to $10 per share and you buy ten shares. The following month, it's back up to $20 per share, your original share price. Have you made or lost money? The stock price has fluctuated, but it ends up back where you started.

The Money Talk

Let's look at the math:

> First month - $100 at $20 per share = 5 shares
> Second month - $100 at $25 per share = 4 shares
> Third month - $100 at $10 per share = 10 shares
> Fourth month - $100 at $20 per share = 5 shares
> Invested $400 and you own 24 shares x $20/
>   share = $480
> This means $480 - $400 invested equals an $80 profit.

These are some wild price swings, but in this case, they're meant to make the math easier to illustrate a point. Many people would assume they had not made any money because the stock price moved up and down, but never really increased. As you can see from the illustration above, that is not the case. That's why dollar cost averaging is so effective.

The benefit of dollar cost averaging goes away if you attempt to time the market, buying more when the market goes up and subsequently, your confidence rises; buying less when the market drops along with your confidence. The best way to do this is to ignore the monkeys and news broadcasters and all the naysayers and stick with your program.

Rain or shine, market up or down, stay with it. It's that simple. If you choose the route of buying individual stocks, you can employ a similar technique. It requires more work, but it's exactly what I do when buying stocks. I first save some money in a regular stock account. When I have enough to justify the price of a trade, I buy a stock. The beautiful thing about owning ten to twenty different stocks is that every time I get money, there are more stocks I like than there is money to spend. I'm never sitting around wondering if I should buy stock. It's like going to a buffet and having difficulty deciding which foods to try. I have discovered by owning many great companies, at least one of them will be unfairly punished for some reason every quarter.

For example, the entire market is steadily rising, but one of my pet companies announced their revenue only increased twenty-one percent; the analyst thought it would be twenty-two percent. The stock price drops, and it presents an excellent buying opportunity.

Sometimes revenue does hit analyst expectations, but the company announces the next quarter's outlook may suffer for various reasons, perhaps torrential flooding in an area where their products are sold, or a record snowfall and people couldn't get to their stores. With the announcement of these stories often come a drop of five to ten percent—and I buy it on sale. If there is a perfectly reasonable explanation as to why sales dropped and I'm satisfied nothing is fundamentally wrong with the company, this is like using a coupon.

Nearly every time I get some cash together, one of my favorite companies has suffered something of this nature and the short-term guys are willing to give me part of a great company at a discount. Other times, the whole market has pulled back and nothing has happened to the company, yet they are all on sale. This is, of course, fine with me. In fact, it's better than fine; I'm ecstatic.

Think of it in this way. Your favorite track star blows out his shoe during a 100-meter sprint. Let's say the sole of his shoe comes off mid stride. The fans in the bleachers speculate he is finished with racing. It's all over for this guy. You, on the other hand, look at the shoe and ask the runner if he is injured. If a doctor examines him and says he is okay, you relax and probably still bet on him in the next race. In fact, you might get great odds because everyone was over reacting when you knew the real story. However, a torn hamstring would be reason to worry. You might decide to agree with the fans in the bleachers. You might even look for a new favorite track star to follow. You would closely monitor the runner's recovery, but you might not bet the farm on him.

Every time a stock drops you are essentially trying to decide if it's a torn hamstring or a blown out shoe. So every time I get enough money together to buy some stock, somebody's shoe has blown out. The stock pulls back five or maybe even ten percent, and I'm very pleased. I am able to buy this stock on sale because of a silly over reaction.

The Money Talk

Some people avoid investing in individual stocks because of the risk. Fair enough, but why do many of those same people move large sums of retirement plan money in and out of the market? I'm not saying that it's impossible for them to be successful using this method, but I am quite skeptical.

If Buffet and Lynch, both investing legends, say they can't time the market, I doubt anyone else's abilities to do so. Often overlooked is that many of these investment plans don't immediately move money upon receiving orders. If a crisis occurs, money can't be moved instantaneously. Transfers can take anywhere from two to twelve hours before the transmission is complete. This lag time makes it impossible to capitalize on late-breaking news.

It's also important to remember the stock market is comprised of thousands of companies and their CEOs, along with millions of people buying and selling stocks based on whims and feelings. Often, facts are overlooked and people act based on an irrational mindset. I prefer the method of researching a particular CEO and the company's sales and products offerings. Then you can make an informed guess as to what that company's share price will do in the future, as opposed to just guessing what millions of traders are going to do.

I don't condemn anyone who day trades their 401(k); it's their money. However, *day trading* isn't much safer than buying individual stocks, if at all. It's actually a lot more difficult. For example, any diversification benefits someone could enjoy from owning hundreds of different stocks is negated by attempting to time the market. Nearly all the benefit they would gain from dollar cost averaging is also wiped out. While it's not impossible to make a profit, you can lose money by holding mostly mutual funds (because they're "safe") and jumping into bonds and treasuries then back to stocks. If you are going to buy mutual funds because they are safer, at least reap the benefits of "safety" and quit trying to time the market.

13

LIFE INSURANCE VERSUS INVESTING

HAVE YOU EVER WONDERED why some people refuse to go skydiving when the odds of death are 1 in 100,000? One study found just eighteen deaths out of 2.2 million jumps in 2007.[30] In other words, their odds of sky jumping success are virtually assured, but most people refuse to do it. However, many of those same people will buy a lottery ticket every week, although odds of winning (about 1 in 175,000,000[31].) virtually assure they won't. It would seem that death is an unacceptable outcome of skydiving, but going home with a few less dollars in their pocket after failing at the lottery is acceptable. I have been skydiving once, and I bought a lottery ticket once; I no longer do either. I bought the lottery ticket because my dad asked me to, and I went skydiving because I thought it would be fun. I'm not advocating or condemning those choices, but I also don't think either are wise.

We don't take chances with choices that leave us with unacceptable outcomes. Leaving my family struggling in the case of my untimely demise is an unacceptable outcome; I hope you share that sentiment. Life insurance is not an investment, nor is it a lottery ticket for loved ones when you die. It's not a means for making money for retirement either. So why do we buy life insurance? Its primary purpose is to replace income in the event of your death.

This aspect of building wealth is often overlooked because people don't want to deal with unpleasant realities. Some don't carry life insurance because they say they don't want to be worth more dead than alive. Most of us don't like to think about dying, but the fact is that ignoring that unpleasant reality will not stop it from happening. However, the thought of my children struggling to stay clothed and fed because it was unpleasant for me to think about death is absurd. You will die eventually. That is not my opinion; it is a fact. You need to ensure your family will be cared for when you die.

Many opinions on this subject exist, but most financial professionals agree you need some type of life insurance.

However, life insurance is:

- **not going to make you die sooner than if you had none**
- **not a lottery ticket for your kids**
- **not an investment**

Many people don't understand these basic principles. A life insurance policy will not cause you to die any sooner. It exists to replace your income so your loved ones don't suffer in the unlikely event of your death. Life insurance is not a wealth-building tool either. Do not buy life insurance so your eighteen-year-old son can drive a Maserati to his first day of college. Buy it so in the event of your death, your family can maintain the standard of living you currently provide for them.

Some people buy **whole-life policies**, which combines insurance with investing. However, there is usually some kind of gimmick involved where you pay in a lot while you are young and healthy. As you get older, this life insurance is going to make you rich. That's what you're told anyway, but it doesn't.

> *You are better off separating your insurance from your investments.*

Life Insurance versus Investing

An associate of mine asked if I would review the life insurance paperwork he received from his employer. He was in his mid-thirties and would have to pay $5,000 per year for twenty-five years. His policy would be worth less than $500,000 by the time he was sixty-nine years old. If he died beforehand, his family would receive a payout of $140,000 for his death benefit; this number would continue to fluctuate every year as he aged.

I did some research for him, discovering he could buy a ***term life*** policy of $500,000 for less than $400 per year. He could then take the additional $4,600 dollars per year he would have invested in the whole life scheme and place it in an index mutual fund. He would accrue over $1,000,000 during the same period in this scenario. He would gain a life insurance policy that provided more money for his family if he died prematurely, and provide him and his family with a lot more wealth if he did not.

Many salesmen try to sell whole life insurance, and they have various complicated and convoluted pitches. Remember, you are better off separating your insurance and investments. Insurance is for protection; investing is to build wealth. Do not confuse these two very different things.

With that said, you probably don't need much (if any) life insurance if:

- **you're single**
- **without children or loved ones who depend on you for financial support**
- **you have sufficient funds to pay for your burial.**

I know unmarried coworkers without children or dependents who are insured to the hilt. These people do not understand the purpose of insurance.

Additionally, if your wife is a stay-at-home mother but provides an invaluable service like caring for your children, you may want to insure her even though she doesn't produce "income." I have life insurance on Lindsey because if she passed away, I would need to hire a caregiver for our children while I went to work. In this case, it's wise to insure someone who does not produce income, but who provides an invaluable service.

The Money Talk

Insurance is for protection; investing is to build wealth.

With that said, our long-term goal should be to do without life insurance. When you are seventy years old, retired, your children are married and self-supporting, you have paid off your house, and have adequate money set aside for your spouse to live on comfortably, then you don't need life insurance. If you aren't producing income or providing an invaluable service to someone, you do not need life insurance. Eventually, you should be self-insured, with everything paid off and your assets producing enough income to support your dependents.

Bottom Line: Life insurance and investing are not equal. Life insurance should be used for replacing your income in case of your unexpected death. Investing should be used to increase your wealth. Keeping these separate will leave you in a much better financial position.

14

STOCKS AND LOTTERY TICKETS

REMEMBER, A STOCK CERTIFICATE is not a lottery ticket. A *stock certificate* is your share of a company. This is basic but misinterpreted logic. Why else would someone sell when the price drops, panicked they will lose more money? The fact that they believe they're losing money is evidence they either misunderstood this simple concept or they are not long-term investors.

For instance, if housing prices started dropping and you discovered your house appraised for $20,000 less than its purchase price five years ago, would you sell it and rent an apartment, waiting until it returns to its original value before you purchase it again? Of course not. That's absurd. But people do this every day with stocks. They buy a stock, and if the price drops twenty percent, they panic and sell it. When the market recovers, they feel safe and buy back in.

Here's another example. You paid $20,000 cash for a car, but a week after you bought it, prices drop and it's now valued at $16,000. Would you run out and sell it for $16,000, then wait for the market to safely recover before you purchased it again at full price? Absolutely not. You would probably ignore this entirely. In fact, if prices dropped substantially, you might even purchase another house or truck with the intention of selling it when the prices came back up. If you viewed stock certificates as ownership of tangible assets (like a car or a house), why would you buy shares of a profitable company, only to sell out when the market pulled back and it's on sale?

Not convinced yet? Look at it this way. You own a trucking company called Truck Inc. The company owns ten delivery trucks. There are ten shares outstanding, so each share represents ten percent of the company. One share equals one truck. Each delivery truck is worth $10,000, and each truck makes $2,000 profit each year. At the end of five years, Truck Inc. buys ten more trucks with the profit it has produced; now there are twenty trucks in total. If you still own just one share of company stock, it is now worth $20,000. Effectively, you have doubled your money, and now own two trucks.

Truck Inc.

> Ten trucks worth $10,000 each ten shares outstanding
>   = $100,000 (company worth)
> Each truck produces $2,000 per year
> Ten trucks x $2,000/year for five years = $100,000 profit
> Truck Inc. buys ten new trucks after five years; twenty
>   trucks at $10,000 per truck
> Company worth = $200,000
> Each share now equals $20,000

If the market pulls back and someone offers you $10,000 for your share of Truck Inc., would you sell it before you "lost" more money? No. In fact, if the owners of the outstanding shares of Truck Inc. offered to sell for $10,000 each, I bet you would buy their shares (assuming the trucks were running as usual, making deliveries and money just like they always had). Indeed, the fundamentals of a business are the important thing.

Like Ben Graham said, "...Price is what you pay; value is what you get."[32]

Obviously, a multi-billion-dollar company is more difficult to navigate than a scenario such as Truck Inc. above, but the principle remains the same. If a company has been profitable for years and has a good long-term track record, it's reasonable to assume that when the entire market pulls back thirty percent, it's just panicked investors. Do your research to be sure your assumption is correct, but it's probably a pretty safe bet.

Publicly-traded companies, by law, must publish their books, balance sheets, profits, and losses by accepted accounting principles. If they aren't doing anything illegal, then it's not unpredictable that if sales and profits are increasing every quarter—and have been for several quarters in a row—the stock's value will eventually increase. In the short-term, a stock's price may not correlate with the stock's value. However, over long periods of time there will be a very close correlation. The disparity in price and value helps us make more money. Even when we can't determine what the stock's exact cost should be, we are relatively certain it will trend upward.

The Gardner brothers say that price is irrelevant if you plan to hold a stock for a couple of decades. I wouldn't say it's completely irrelevant, but I don't place a lot of importance on it. Does it really matter if you buy in at a ten percent discount if it will be worth five times the purchase price in fifteen years? I'd be willing to pay a ten percent premium every time if I was guaranteed that kind of return.

Much confusion exists around what constitutes a high stock price. Amazon is currently trading around $742 as of today, but Amazon produces a lot of money. That does not mean the stock is necessarily expensive. Often when someone says a stock is expensive, they are referring to the Price to Earnings *(P/E)* ratio or some other metric. Usually when analysts say a stock is expensive, they mean its price relative to the amount of money the company is likely to produce in the future is not in line with how much the stock costs.

With that in mind, realize that one analyst may call a stock that costs $10 with a P/E of 100 really expensive. Another stock that costs $100 with a P/E of twelve is cheap. If you are buying stocks without doing research, it's much like shooting craps. Your odds of being successful over a long period of time are slim if you select your stocks by throwing darts at a board. *Do your homework.* This fundamental understanding is one thing that makes investing so profitable. Don't be like people who try making a quick buck off a stock tip they received from their brother-in-law. They do no research; they just take the leap. Investing is a gamble to some extent, but the odds are tilted steeply in your favor if you do your homework. The only way it's a sure bet is if you have insider information. That is illegal, so I would never advise it. With that said, it's not shooting craps or playing roulette if you put in the work and know what you are buying.

Every time I hear someone claiming to be able to time the market, I think of an old man named Zef Cane. Zef lived in Bastrop, the small Louisiana town where I grew up. A bachelor for his entire life, Mr. Cane was a bit of a local legend. He was still driving in his '90s, stowing a half pint of whiskey in one back pocket and a can of Skoal chewing tobacco in the other. Mr. Cane regularly drove down the Crossett Highway at twenty-five miles per hour in his truck. At that breakneck speed, he didn't dare turn his head to spit tobacco out the truck window. Rather than take his eyes off the road, he would spit right on the dash. There were usually at least ten cars behind Zef, waiting for a straightaway to pass him.

Many ladies, such as my beloved Mamaw Gussy, did not approve of Mr. Cane's proclivities. After all, Bastrop was in the "Bible Belt" of the United States. Liquor and tobacco use, though common, were frowned upon.

Mr. Cane finally went to live in the nursing home when he was nearly ninety-two years old. My Mamaw Franklin worked there and asked Zef how he liked it. Mr. Cane replied that had he known how many single women were at the nursing home, he would have moved there years earlier. He was quite a character.

Mr. Cane lived for several years at the nursing home before he passed away. Mamaw Gussy was rumored to have said, "That whiskey and snuff finally got him." Indeed, after almost a hundred years, alcohol and tobacco did finally kill Zef Cane.

I regularly see articles forecasting a stock market collapse, and even a few envisioning a market boom. Or I see someone who has predicted the last three market collapses offering to share their insights as to when the next one is coming "for a small fee, and you can become rich too." The part they conveniently omit is that although they got four market collapses right, they predicted another twenty-five market collapses that didn't happen. We all know even a broken clock is right twice a day. Will you eventually be right about the market tanking? Yes. But staying out of the market for all those years because of the impending collapse will be more financially damaging than weathering those storms.

> *Smile when you read a headline that says "Investors lose as market falls." Edit it in your mind to "Dis-investors lose as market falls—but investors gain." Though writers often forget this truism, there is a buyer for every seller and what hurts one necessarily helps the other.*
>
> —Warren Buffett

Bottom Line: Do not try to time the stock market. Stocks aren't lottery tickets, so do your research.

15

BACK TO BASICS

Everyone must become financially literate. Why? Because almost no one in our country will receive a retirement pension. Very few employers will send you a retirement check equivalent to sixty percent of your salary for the rest of your life. So, if you'd rather not be eating dog food in retirement, you must learn how to prepare for it yourself.

Hopefully you now have an understanding of saving and investing, and you are ready to get started. Mr. Lynch is a huge proponent of buying what you know. Lynch frequently asked his wife and three daughters questions about what they like to eat, what brands their friends wore, and where they liked to shop. He'd wait in the mall while they shopped, carefully watching the stores they said were popular. He wouldn't automatically buy the stock, of course, but if it proved to be a popular store where management was responsible and ethical, then the stock was generally worth buying.

Again, this goes back to what we discussed in the previous chapter: *a stock is not a lottery ticket.* You don't necessarily run out and buy the company just because you like its products. Although it's more complicated than that, it's a great place to start. Think about that for a while. What are some products you love? What is your favorite grocery store? Beer? Car? Clothing store? Are they publicly traded? If you really love their products, and your friends, kids, and everyone else around you is using them, there is a good chance that company makes a lot of sales.

Many people want to buy stock in a company in which they have no knowledge. Don't take the hot stock tip from the guy at the gym. Instead, lean on your knowledge of products you use and love. Though you may not realize it yet, your unique personal knowledge will help you find good stock investments.

For example, I worked as a city mail carrier in a small New Mexico town during the late '90s and early 2000s. I began to notice how many people on my mail route received bright red envelopes from some company called Netflix. While it may be hard to imagine now, this company would send a DVD in the mail because there was no such thing as online streaming. Viewers could keep the DVD for as long as they wanted, only returning it when they were ready for another video. Then, Netflix would mail another movie title of the customer's choosing. It may seem like a cumbersome system, but remember, their main competitors were Blockbuster and Movie Gallery.

These companies required a customer to drive to the store and sort through hundreds of movie titles before choosing one to take home. The customer would pay and leave with a DVD or VHS tape (gasp). If you didn't return the movie within two to three days, you had to pay excessive late charges every day until you returned it.

It's obvious which business model won out here. Although I saw those DVD envelopes every day on my mail route, I didn't know enough about the stock market to capitalize on the trend. When I taught myself how to invest several years later, I managed to capitalize on Netflix stock. Had I started researching stocks and investing earlier though, I would have made so much more.

Split-adjusted back in 2002 while I was delivering mail, Netflix was trading for just under $1 per share. It recently closed at $90.79 per share, with a split-adjusted all-time high projection of $123.33 per share by 2016. That qualifies as a "90-bagger" in Lynch speak. I eventually bought Netflix at $16.64 per share, and sold it after making my money back many times over, but nowhere near a 90-**bagger**. I then bought it back later at an even higher price, and it has doubled again. This is one of those times in which I wanted to kick myself as an investor. I should not complain because I made quite a lot of money from Netflix. I paid for a couple of hunting trips to Africa, paid cash for my wife's vehicle, and used some of the proceeds to finish paying off our house. Those were all wonderful things.

As I said, I should be thankful. However, I can't help but think how many nice houses and new cars I could have bought with the earnings made if I had just held on to that investment. If I had bought in 2002 and held it, how much greater would my profit have been?

What I learned is that you will never buy at the bottom or sell at the very top. You will always leave money on the table; get used to the idea. But don't sell a great company just because it has gone up several times and you have made a lot of money from it. The same method applies if the stock drops and you think you're losing money. What you spent on a stock has no bearing whatsoever on its worth. You only sell a company when the fundamentals are falling apart.

In my early years of investing, I bought a horrible stock. I spent years waiting for it to gain value while the fundamentals deteriorated. I learned this lesson: If you can't list in a few minutes why you own a company's stock, you should not own it. On the other hand, if the fundamentals are still solid, don't sell just because you have made a lot of money that you are scared to lose. I have made a lot of money from investing in companies I personally use every day. High performers have been Google, Netflix, Amazon, Apple, and Under Armour. I use products from these companies nearly every day.

Keep in mind that any company experiencing crazy growth will eventually expand in size, which in turn slows overall growth. If it goes up one hundred times in fourteen years, it will grow from a billion-dollar small-cap to an enormous large-cap. This is our end goal. We may have to sell the stock and move the money somewhere else. At some point, the company becomes so large that growth slows, but that is a good problem. I think people spend too much time "number crunching." While that should not be completely ignored, it's not everything. If everyone uses a product and seem to love it, start research from there. Be aware if people appear to sour on a product; it could be time to sell that stock. Although it may be a minor hiccup, it still bears investigation.

I remember when Movie Gallery and Blockbuster were battling it out with Netflix. Judging from the number of angry customers at both stores, it was apparent who was losing the battle. Nearly everyone I knew was angry about paying a $20-$60 accrued late charge because they forgot to return a movie on time. It didn't matter if someone's husband had inadvertently lodged the movie under the car seat or a kid had misplaced it. The store extended no mercy. When the movie was eventually found (one week or one month later), an exorbitant late charge was still applied. The businesses operated as credit card companies do now. They relied on not only rental income but the punitive charges too.

When Netflix became available, most people were all too eager to jump ship and start receiving those red envelopes in the mail. When I finally did buy Netflix, it was obvious that Blockbuster and Movie Gallery were going to lose. Had I owned their stock, I would have known to sell it long before their balance sheet began to suffer. That is the beauty of having personal knowledge of the industry where you purchase stock. If things are going well or going badly, you will often know long before the professional number crunchers do.

Are you beginning to understand why buying stock in an industry you know nothing about is risky business? You are essentially viewing the same set of numbers every Wall Street professional is looking at and trying to beat them at their own game. The size of a company is referred to as ***market capitalization***. Smaller companies can double and triple in size rather quickly; a behemoth like Apple cannot. Of course, Apple can grow and produce a lot of capital, but having a current market cap of around $600 billion makes it difficult for them to double in size. Larger companies tend to be safer, but they give up growth for safety. You don't want a pathetic penny stock either, so strive for something between the two.

- Large cap = $10 billion or larger (Amazon, Apple, Starbucks)
- Mid-cap = $2-$10 billion (Cognex, Casey's)
- Small-cap = less than $2 billion (Duluth Trading Company)

Let's say a pharmaceutical company markets a great drug, and they sell $10 million worth this year. The company already sells $20 billion worth of other drugs, so this $10 million-dollar bump doesn't affect their bottom line. However, if a small company with a market cap of $200 million gains $10 million in profits, it becomes a huge leap. Context is important here. Market capitalization values are subjective terms, but this is generally considered correct circa 2016. Throughout your research, you will hear terms such as *mega-cap* and *micro-cap*. Don't get too wrapped up in those details. Just remember that smaller companies can generally grow faster than larger companies, but if they are too small, they usually struggle more when a recession hits. Again, picking a middle ground is usually better.

Don't try to compete with Wall Street professionals by poring over balance sheets. They look at many factors, one of which is inventory buildup. Companies can try to make their financials look good by carrying a lot of inventory at too high of a price. If their inventory builds up too quickly, it may mean that their product is not selling well. If it's not, they might have to eventually mark the prices down to a fraction just to get rid of it. In the short term, it looks like they are doing great because it shows they have ten million dollars' worth of product in their warehouses but if they eventually must mark the price down on those products and only receive one million dollars when they sell.

I really like the Motley Fool because they put in the legwork of going through the books. Once I owned a stock they had recommended for purchase. Then they suggested selling it because someone involved with the company was using some shady accounting that, while legal, could lend itself to cooking the books. The Motley Fool discovered this because they have people more knowledgeable than I looking over balance sheets. I don't know much about accounting and I don't care to learn. I prefer to let the people at the Motley Fool do the accounting because they are much better at it than I can ever hope to be. They also provide this service at a very reasonable price.

While accounting is not my strong suit, observation is. You have the same advantage as a regular investor and it's what Peter Lynch advocates. You must play to your strengths. If I am going to compete with anyone—in this case it's over money in the stock market—I need to play off my strengths and use their weaknesses to my advantage.

For instance, if I was going to make a bet with someone—my ability verses theirs—and I could pick any activity I wanted, I wouldn't challenge a mixed martial arts enthusiast to a fistfight and I wouldn't challenge a long-distance runner to a marathon. Instead, I might challenge the mixed martial artist to a game of chess or the long-distance runner to a weight lifting match. I might get my tail kicked anyway, but I would have much better odds of success. It's much the same way in stocks.

An accountant is more likely to find something fishy in the books than I am, so I don't try to beat a Wall Street analyst in this realm. I use my powers of observation and pay the Motley Fool to dig through the books, thus using their strengths and my own as well.

In our capitalist system, a *publicly-traded company* is somehow connected to nearly everything you wear, eat, drink, drive, play, or do for recreation. A publicly traded company is one in which you can buy shares of stock in their business. The shoes you wear are likely produced by a publicly traded company (think Nike and Under Armour); the rubber in the shoes is likely produced from petroleum; that petroleum was drilled somewhere then transported somewhere else; it was refined somewhere; it took energy to manufacture the shoes and labor and the tools that were used to make it all happen. It took trucks, power lines, petroleum, a pipeline, copper, iron, and a huge assortment of other businesses to produce that pair of shoes. Each one of these companies is a chance for you to make money. Those who work in trucking notice when a number of trucks are purchased and there are a ton of new trucks on the road. You might notice all of these trucks are made by GM and that their sales are likely to explode. That's observation.

Those who work for a power company know when power lines are installed and the company must buy loads of copper that is more expensive by the day. You might want to check out a company mining copper. That's observation. And when everyone wears Under Armour shoes and drinks Starbucks every morning, there are endless other possible opportunities. That's observation.

This is what we are looking for—*this* is our advantage. By the time the accountant realizes this stock is going through the roof, you've already noticed how everyone seems to love Starbucks. It's not something you read in a report; you *observed* the trend before most of the professionals. This is the equivalent of challenging a fifty-year old fat guy to a foot race. You are using your strengths to your advantage and not playing his game.

Stockbrokers versus Analysts

For the most part, stockbrokers are not analysts. Occasionally, analysts become brokers and vice versa, but often stockbrokers rely entirely on analysts. They are often given credit for being masters of the stock market, and some probably are, but if that's the case you won't have access to them. They often work for or run **hedge funds** for wealthy people who pay for their advice. Most people don't understand this and believe the broker has a huge advantage over them for picking stocks, but this is unusual.

I realized this some years ago on a very personal level. I had read some Peter Lynch books and I knew he often wanted a ballpark value of a stock in case the company was liquidated. I was anxious to learn this. I had no Internet access at the time so I had my uncle, a residential contractor, send me the financials for a couple of companies I had read about. These included basic details such as balance sheets and income statements. I then scheduled an appointment to meet with a stockbroker from a locally operated brokerage chain.

I was impressed upon entering the office. It was very clean, and even the secretaries were dressed professionally. The company's investing brochures were top notch. But it spiraled downhill from there. I walked into the broker's office and explained that I was new to investing in individual stocks but had some money in mutual funds that I could move if so inclined. I then produced the balance sheets and income statements and explained I didn't want him to make me an accountant; I just wanted him to explain how he personally analyzed a stock to determine its valuation. I was simply hoping he would review some financials with me.

The broker looked absolutely dumbfounded. Firstly, he wanted to see the pages I had printed out. Then, he turned to his computer in a panic, frantically typing and searching. After three or four minutes of this, he told me he wasn't sure if he had access to the financials and wanted to know if my uncle worked on Wall Street. I explained that my uncle was, in fact, a contractor who knew almost nothing about stocks. He then broke down and told me the truth.

"I don't actually do much research on stocks myself; we have analysts who do that. I usually just look at whatever they are recommending, and that's what I recommend." He then brightened up, took out a pen out and scribbled a crude chart resembling the workings of a third-grader. The chart had two peaks and three troughs.

"This stock I know of has gone from $40 up to $64 and back down to $40, then back to $64. Now it's back down to $40. It's General Electric and I think it's going to go back to $64."

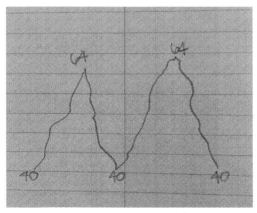

Very near an exact rendition of his graph

121

The Money Talk

I sat stunned for a few minutes. This guy, a "professional money manager," was doodling like a kid with a crayon, while I was trying to learn how to invest. I left not knowing anymore about stocks than I did when I walked in. He seemed to be more of a salesman than a money manager. While I'm sure many brokers are knowledgeable investors, this one clearly was not.

This brings me to another point. Historically, stockbrokers have had no fiduciary standard. That means if they can get you to buy and sell, they can make money while you are losing your shirt. Educate yourself. They are not all wizards of Wall Street.

Bottom Line: Do your research; seek to purchase stocks in a company you know and love. Companies somewhere in the middle are generally a better pick for beginning investors who desire long-term profit. Not all people involved in finance and money management are good at what they do.

16

WHAT'S NEXT

BY NOW, WE HAVE learned some investing basics and identified a few companies we love. What's next? As I have said earlier, I subscribe to the Motley Fool Stock Advisor. I am not an employee, nor is this a plug for their service. I have a lot of respect for David and Tom Gardner. Although Tom's long-term Stock Advisor picks trail David's, there is a good reason. Tom is looking for "rule makers," while David prefers "rule breakers." Consequently, David often recommends smaller, fast-growing companies while Tom prefers larger, stable, slow-growing companies. Whichever brother you side with depends on your risk tolerance, but both are excellent.

When the Gardner brothers analyze the financials of a company, they look at many different factors. For instance, they research whether a company is cutting their research and development budget for no apparent reason. If you are dealing with a technology company, that detail would be troubling because they could be cutting costs to prop up their earnings. This short-term fix would hide the problem for another quarter, but it could be time to consider selling. I once received a sell alert from Motley Fool, who thought there was too much potential for shady accounting by a company accountant who was engaging in a legal and generally accepted accounting principle. This was great insight, and honestly, the type of research I hate doing. I despise digging through financial details, crunching numbers, and attempting to figure out what it all means. This is why I like the Motley Fool so much. I can look through their buy list with confidence, knowing they have invested time in researching the financials of the companies they recommend. To me, it's absolutely worth the $200 per year they charge for their Stock Advisor service. That works out to less than $20 per month. You probably spend that much eating out or buying Starbucks coffee every week. It truly is some of the best money I have ever spent and I highly recommend it to anyone. If I research a stock I personally like and use, and then discover it on Motley Fool's best-buy list, I'm quite confident I can make money. It only becomes a question of how much.

It's not unusual for people to become intimidated, eyes glazing over, when they listen to Lynch explain how to dissect a balance sheet. Why not pay someone else to do this for me? I don't buy stock blindly because the Gardner brothers include it on their list; I still conduct my own research for extra assurance because I want to justify my purchase. After all, it is my money on the line.

You are certainly not limited to using the Motley Fool's Advisor service, but if you review David's long-term track record, it is hard to be unimpressed. Monthly, each brother selects one stock he would buy if he could only choose one. They each also have five starter stocks. These are great stocks for beginners to purchase and hold for a long period of time. Then, they each select their five best buys every month. These are stocks previously named as a pick of the month that are now selling for a very good price. Sometimes, the stock lists overlap and stocks can be recommended again as a pick of the month. This leads to some duplication, meaning a stock could be listed as a pick of the month, a starter, and a best buy now. However, that is rarely the case. Generally, you have about twenty-two stocks to choose from when they release their list. Of those, there are typically five or more that I personally like and use.

Another benefit of Motley Fool is the ability to review their recommendations from years past. Their running total is tracked from 2002 (when they began) until now. Upon reviewing this list, you'll find David recommended Amazon back in September 2002. At that time, no one thought this "Interwebs" thing was going to be a vital method for shopping. But now, the stock price has gone up over 4,000 percent in that timeframe. David also suggested Activision as a buy in 2003, and it has increased about 2,000 percent since that time. Additionally, David recommended Priceline in May 2004; it has returned about 5,000 percent since then. Finally, he encouraged buying Netflix in October 2004; it has returned around 3,500 percent. When you are "right" that often, you can also be wrong a lot and still have a great portfolio. However, David is not mistaken often, so he has a superb long-term track record.

Bottom Line: I am not interested in painstakingly researching a company's financial history. I would rather pay someone, such as Motley Fool's Stock Advisor service, to do this for me. Unless you plan to dissect a company's financials yourself, you need to find someone who will. This is a crucial key in determining which stocks to buy.

17

JUSTIFICATION: A SYNOPSIS

By now, we realize that personal knowledge of a company's products can help guide us toward choosing which stocks to purchase. We also understand that knowing the company has sound financials is equally important, even if we aren't the ones scrutinizing their books. Now, we need to dig a little more. I like to do this by setting up a mock portfolio via Yahoo Finance. It's an excellent free resource. While it's easiest if you already have a Yahoo email account, you can still use the tool. You'll just need to create an account before getting started. The entire setup process takes about five minutes. You can also load the Yahoo Finance app to your smart phone and it will track your investments up to the minute.

Next, conduct some research on a few companies. Write a brief synopsis stating why you think they are great companies to purchase. Why do you think they will perform well? I usually copy and paste the articles used as supporting information to my report. I find out who is the CEO and look for a glass door rating. Their background, and if they own the stock. I find out who the company's competitors are and if they have an edge over them called a "moat". I then write about my own personal experience with the company and its products. I talk to people wearing or using the company's products. I get feedback about why they and their families like the products. I then look to make sure *Motley Fool* recommends them.

Yahoo Finance lists almost every recent article written on the stocks you track. There, you can find stories from *Zacks*, *The Street*, the *Wall Street Journal*, and other financial sources. According to Lynch, the synopsis should be written in language a fifth-grader can understand, and short enough to keep said fifth-grader from getting bored. I use all this information to draw my conclusions. I copy and paste articles I read that both support my position and run counter to it. If I find articles contrary to my position, I must present a legitimate argument as to why I believe they are wrong.

This is an important step for a few reasons. One is that several years from now, I may not remember why I thought so highly of the stock. If you keep ten stocks or so, you probably won't be able to remember why you thought they were a great buy in another four to five years. The second reason is to remove my emotions from the decision-making process. "I really feel good about this one." is not a legitimate reason to buy a company's stock. I have had people read my stock synopsis and ask if I was trying to convince myself it was a good buy. Yes, that is exactly what I am doing. If I can't justify why I'm buying it or why I will continue to own it, then perhaps it may be time to sell. Don't worry if writing is not your strong point either. Perfect grammar and punctuation are unimportant. Your synopsis just needs to be clear enough to jog your memory when you look back. Be sure to include the date.

This is an example of my stock synopsis:

> *Amazon is one of my favorite companies to own. Jeff Bezos, the head, is like an evil genius with ever-developing schemes to rule the world of retail. They are involved in everything you can possibly imagine. They announced about five weeks ago that they were going to lease twenty 767 cargo jets to start their own freight-delivery service in the U.S. In response to rising delivery costs, they have been doing some of their own delivery services. They have done some experimentation with drones to expedite the process. They are starting a new Prime service that you can pay for on a monthly*

The Money Talk

basis, as well as a standalone streaming service you can purchase without buying a Prime membership.

The Echo is a newer product. It is a type of electronic assistant that you speak to in order to operate electronics around your home or order stuff from Amazon. AWS cloud computing is going nuts and creating a lot of revenue. Their customers are accusing them of copying products and selling them on Amazon. Allegedly they can track what's selling well, and then produce it under their own label (Amazon Basics), effectively cutting out the middleman. Keep in mind this was a company that started out selling books. My wife loves the company, and we order something from them nearly every week. We buy groceries locally, but most of the other things we buy are online. Amazon is killing brick-and-mortar stores; Wal-Mart is getting left in the dust. There has been a slight pullback lately in the stock price, but Amazon is killing it. I'm not selling mine anytime soon.

I write a synopsis about once every quarter, usually just before or after company earnings are reported. I've owned Amazon for about eight years and have made around a 560 percent return on my original investment. I have purchased it on more than one occasion; remember what I said about buying stock on sale? Whenever I felt the stock was unfairly punished I bought some more, making my total return closer to 393 percent. Why would I do this? Although Amazon's stock has increased several times, I may purchase more if the stock drops for some reason.

Sometimes skittish investors read a news story that spooks them into selling. In this case, perhaps a **start-up** is threatening to run Amazon out of business, or Wal-Mart is making a comeback. If my own experience tells me differently and I can support my position with facts, then it may be time to buy when others are selling.

Another way I set myself up for success is by budgeting a fixed amount to transfer directly into my stock accounts. When I have enough saved to justify a broker fee, I buy a stock; this usually occurs every five to six weeks.

I review all of the stocks I've researched to find the best sale. If a stock reported growth of twenty percent and analysts were expecting twenty-one percent, the stock price might get hammered. If I uncover a legitimate reason to account for the "miss", and there is nothing wrong with the company's fundamentals, I buy the stock. If the company is experiencing a temporary setback because they are building new stores and expanding, it's completely normal for their profits to suffer in the short term. If I decide they are expanding at a reasonable pace, then there is a good chance it's an opportune time to buy when the price drops.

Often, several great companies are unfairly penalized by missed earnings reports. In this case, my biggest challenge becomes choosing which company I would rather buy. I liken this feeling to walking into a gun store that has an AR-15 rifle, 1911 pistol, and an over-and-under 12-gauge shotgun, and they're all twenty percent off their regular price. I can't decide which one I want more. When I am ready to purchase a stock at any given time, of the seventeen I'm currently tracking, at least three will have experienced some sort of unjustified pullback. It's a wonderful thing most investors don't understand. You must embrace that volatility and see it for what it is-opportunity. Yes, you may already own $30,000 of that stock, just like I may already own four shotguns. But if the store slashes the shotgun's price by thirty percent, I don't view it as though I lost money on the four shotguns I already own. I see that as receiving the fifth one at a great deal.

If I have conducted my research well, prices will inevitably increase on both the stock and the shotguns. This volatility is why we can make money, so embrace it.

> **Whether we're talking about socks or stocks, I like buying quality merchandise when it is marked down.**
> —Warren Buffett

I also like to research the company's CEO. I usually do this via Motley Fool, as they will often post the CEO's glass-door rating. This determines what the employees think of their CEO. Often, this proves crucial, as companies in booming industries go broke every day because of poor leadership. There are also companies booming in falling industries that prosper because of good leadership.

If you buy stock in a company whose CEO previously turned around several failing companies, you can be confident he will do well with your company. If you get a leader like Steve Jobs, Jeff Bezos, or Reed Hastings, you can be confident they will improve the company's growth and bottom line. Because I don't try to figure out an individual stock's worth anymore, I watch and wait for something to happen. When a stock I love gets unfairly punished, I use the opportunity to add to my position.

A great growth stock might be on the rise for years. It might jump up several times while many sit on the sidelines waiting for a price pullback. Sometimes, pundits write daily articles telling you how overpriced the stock is, and you watch in horror as it goes up several times. I follow the Motley Fool's advice and move forward with a purchase if it is on their best-buy list. I do this even if the other "professionals" say the stock is overpriced. I will also add to that position if there is a fifteen to twenty percent pullback because the company missed earnings. If the stock was a deal at $100 per share, and they miss earnings by a couple of cents or profit projections by one to two percent, it drops to $90. If they were expecting revenue to increase by seventeen percent, and it only grew by fifteen percent, I count that as a good thing. The stock is now selling for a ten percent discount.

I do my research. If the fundamentals are sound, then I consider the stocks to be on sale. I like to incorporate the Gardner brothers' philosophy of buying a great growth stock, even if it's a little "overpriced," then use Buffett's philosophy to add to my position when the stock price drops and is a great deal. You'll find in the reading list I provided that while the authors don't always agree, they are all legendary investors and money managers. I encourage you to develop a style that plays on your strengths coupled with their teachings. You may not agree with everything Buffett does, or everything Lynch and the Gardner brothers do; in fact, you necessarily will not because not all their ideas are exactly alike. You can, however, still tailor a system that works best for you, choosing the techniques from each of these legendary investors, making a system of your own. You can glean a lot of knowledge from each one of them, making sound investment decisions based on their wisdom and advice.

There are certain areas of investment that I avoid at all costs. I do not invest money in sectors where the government is heavily involved, such as a sector with excessive government regulation. The government is involved in nearly everything to some degree these days, but they are especially involved in energy, healthcare, and banking. I've observed that too many rules are made haphazardly, which can make or break businesses. I'm not going to go in to politics, but I will say that if the government gets too involved, winners and losers seem to become arbitrary pawns in a big chess game and a *free market economy* does not work properly. This makes for dangerous investing if you are not an insider. I am not, so to avoid these pitfalls, I generally avoid these sectors.

Making financial decisions based on feelings is silly. How I feel is based on many factors not related to finance at all. What I've eaten or if I've had enough sleep or if my kids are sick all have an effect on my outlook. I "feel" less optimistic in general if any of those things are out of sorts, but I'm pretty sure none of them will affect how much money a company produces or how many sales they have. Try keeping this in mind when you hear about the latest reason why the "world is going to melt down". Try to completely divorce yourself from your feelings and make a calm, rational, informed decision.

Bottom Line: Get clear on why you're investing in the companies you choose; keep a written synopsis that you can refer to in the future. Volatility and irrational behavior are what allows you to make money in the stock market; embrace it. Be careful investing in heavily regulated sectors.

18

A MOCK PORTFOLIO

IF YOU WERE GOING to do something that you deemed important, but also potentially dangerous if you failed, how would you start? For example, you have never been skiing, but decide you're going to take a stab at it. Would you just load up the family and drive to a ski lodge that day? Would you walk in to the ski shop and buy the most expensive pair of skis you could afford? Would you purchase season lift tickets, and hop the first lift to the mountain top? Would you then jump off at the first pair of double black diamonds you saw and start your ski adventure?

I'm guessing most people would take a more measured approach. They would talk to a few friends and find out where to go. They might research skiing and talk to others who enjoy it. Perhaps they would consider taking a trip to the closest ski area and observe others skiing. Finally, they might try out the bunny slope or hire a ski instructor for the morning. While they might eventually end up on a double black diamond, it would most likely take multiple trips and practice before they had the skills and confidence to do so.

Take my advice and start on the bunny slopes. Do some reading, talk to a few people who invest, and then build a mock portfolio. Rolling your life savings into a stock account you day trade is the equivalent of jumping on the double black diamond trail when you've never been skiing a day in your life. You now know how to conduct stock research, choose stocks, and write a synopsis of the company. Let's say you use your mock *Yahoo Finance* portfolio to invest an imaginary amount of money. Take $10,000 for example. Divide this amount between at least five stocks, preferably ten to fifteen. Why? Lynch recommends a minimum of five stocks because of those five, one will experience some unforeseen problem (CEO quits, accounting scandal, new competitor, etc.). Three will do marginally well and will make some money. And one stock is going to blow your socks off. In fact, Lynch says even finding one really good stock every decade is enough to make you very wealthy. On the other end of the spectrum, you don't want to own more stocks than you can manage. Don't use the shotgun approach; we want to be very deliberate with our selections.

If you have a full-time job, finding out why one of your stocks dropped or rose more than five percent on any given day becomes rather challenging if you have too many to research. Once you have made your selections, find out the current price per share. If it's $100 per share, you can buy ten shares (10 x $100 per share = $1,000). Let's say your next favorite stock is $50 dollars per share, so you buy twenty shares (20 x $50 per share = $1,000). Keep doing this until you have ten stocks with an imaginary $1,000 in each stock. Remember, stock prices will be irregular. You may have $1,123 in one stock and $897 in another. Get as close as possible to $1,000 per stock.

This is an example of what a mock portfolio should look like with the minimum five stocks and $5,000 fictitious dollars to invest. The tabs underneath list current news stories on the stocks included in the portfolio. When you have your portfolio completely set up, you will see a list of current finance articles relating to the companies you purchased. This makes it convenient to browse and see the most up-to-date news as it relates to your stock holdings. For instance, if you bought Amazon and it increases or decreases ten percent in value that day, there will most certainly be an article addressing why that happened. This is a free, quick, and easy resource, so take advantage of it.

My Portfolios S&P 500 -0.02%   Dow -0.06%   Nasdaq +0.15%

book ▼   Edit   Reorder   Download   Set alerts   Add/edit holdings | Create new   Manage all

| Basic | DayWatch | Performance | recent news | Real-Time | Fundamentals | Detailed | ⚙ Add Custom View |

Enter Symbol   ⊕ Add Symbol   Customize current view

SYMBOL	TIME & PRICE		CHG & % CHG	VOLUME	MORE INFO	
AMZN	04:00pm EDT	784.48	-4.39 -0.56%	2,379,027	Chart, News, Stats, Options, Board	×
AAPL	04:00pm EDT	108.38	+0.68 +0.63%	42,034,985	Chart, News, Stats, Options, Board	×
NFLX	04:00pm EDT	99.15	-0.94 -0.94%	6,434,302	Chart, News, Stats, Options, Board	×
UA	04:04pm EDT	39.92	+0.99 +2.54%	8,192,397	Chart, News, Stats, Options, Board	×
FB	04:00pm EDT	131.05	+1.32 +1.02%	27,690,160	Chart, News, Stats, Options, Board	×

Recent News

Today

AAPL   Everything Apple just launched at today's massive event at Quartz Wed 4:16pm

AAPL   So, Apple ditched the headphone jack. Get over it! at CNBC Wed 4:12pm

AAPL FB   Apple Debuts New iPhones And Apple Watch at Investopedia Wed 4:11pm

AAPL   Apple Inc.'s iPhone 7 and its 10 Flashy Features Won't Move AAPL Stock at US News & World Report Wed 4:16pm

AAPL   Nintendo's U.S.-listed shares surge as games come to iPhone and Apple Watch at MarketWatch Wed 4:10pm

AAPL   Requiem for the iPhone's tangled earbud cord at San Jose Mercury News Wed 4:07pm

If you hit the performance tab, you can track your return over a long period of time, or daily and up to the minute.

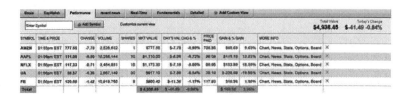

A mock portfolio allows you to track your individual returns on each stock as well as your entire portfolio. It is constantly updated during the day, so you can see current returns or your return since purchasing it. You can view how much money you have in each stock, as well as the dollar amount gained or lost that day and since its purchase. One thing I like most about this process is that you can create mock portfolios as well as track real accounts you own elsewhere. The advantage here is that even if someone hacked into your *Yahoo* email account, they cannot access your real account

134

information. If you are traveling and log in to a public computer, you can see the information you require, without worrying about someone wrongfully accessing your financial accounts.

Another advantage to this system is you don't risk real money until you are confident you understand the investing process. If you begin managing a mock portfolio and decide a few months later it's not for you, you haven't lost a dime and you can close the account. I know a lot of people who want to skip this part and use real money immediately; if you have the stomach for it that's okay, but many do not. Some people put real money in, and then suffer a loss; or it grows too slowly and they become disenchanted. Many folks say investing isn't interesting to them. Unfailingly, it becomes *very* interesting when they have a few thousand dollars invested. The more zeroes, the more interesting it gets.

Once you have generated enough interest, knowledge, confidence, and money, you are ready to begin investing. I like using my USAA investment account because of the ease with which I can invest. I have used Scottrade and Edward Jones investing services, and they work well too. However, I much prefer having my banking and brokerage accounts in one place. It's convenient. I have USAA stock accounts for both of our children. If they receive a gift of money, I deposit it from any mobile device to my checking account. I can then transfer it directly into their stock account, all in a matter of one minute. With other services, it was an arduous process of depositing the check, writing another check, mailing it to the investing service, then waiting for them to receive it before they could initiate a stock purchase. My time is worth a lot, and USAA simplifies this process greatly.

Bottom Line: Build your confidence and your knowledge by first creating a mock portfolio. When you are ready, locate an investment service that meets your needs for buying and selling stocks.

19

A LONG-TERM PLAN

Where do you want to be when you retire? We touched on this earlier, but let's dig a little deeper now. For easy figuring, let's say you make $100,000 a year now and you would like to keep the same lifestyle when you retire. How much will it take to reach that goal? Let's be clear: at some point, you will need to move a sizable portion of money out of the stock market. Financial planners generally recommend the following equation to help you choose the amount: 100 minus your age equals the amount you should have in stocks.

If you are sixty, it looks like this:

> 100 - 60 years old = 40% in the market, 40% stocks,
> 60% bonds

A little less than half my holdings should be in stocks. The remaining sixty percent should be invested in something more stable, such as bonds, because the younger you are the longer you can wait out a stock market correction. As you age, you move further toward stability and a steady income. I do not necessarily agree with the formula, but it is often touted as a good model. I prefer to put more in stocks.

If interest rates are very low the return on bonds will be very low. For the last few years, interest rates have been abysmal, so bonds have been shunned for that reason. Where would you like to be? Let's crunch a few numbers and get a little better idea. Let's say you will only receive a retirement from Social Security and your investment returns. Hopefully the Federal Reserve will quit manipulating interest soon so you can once again make money in bonds. But if not, you need to find a stable investment vehicle that will return six percent on your investment.

I am leaning towards purchasing a rental property. We briefly ran over some figures earlier in the book about not running out of money in retirement. As you age, you may not have time to wait out an extended stock market pullback, or you may not have any kids or loved ones with whom you wish to leave money. You need to customize your plan to fit your individual needs. The basic idea below is for someone like me who has children. It can be adjusted to fit your needs. You will retire at sixty with $1,500,000 in investments and you are completely debt-free. You should place part of your money in an investment to produce income, and part of it in another investment to preserve purchasing power. This protects you from inflation.

If you have inexpensive hobbies and want to leave an inheritance for your children, you might do something like this:

> At sixty, you have $1,500,000 total
> Move $750,000 into stocks
> Move $750,000 into bonds or rentals
> $750,000 in stocks will average ten percent
> $750,000 in bonds (or rental properties) x 6% annual
>   return = $45,000 per year to live on in retirement.

This is approximately $3,750 per month before taxes. If you received $1,000 per month from Social Security, you'll have $4,750 per month, or about $57,000 per year.

Remember the Rule of 72? Let's use it to roughly figure that by sixty-seven, the $750,000 in stocks will have doubled. You now have $1.5 million in stocks. Depending on your health, long-term goals, and other priorities, you can move money.

Let's say you are healthy and your parents are still alive. At this point, you might need to worry more about preserving capital. So, you move $500,000 from the stock account to your bond account. This would change your allowance and thus your lifestyle.

At sixty-seven, you have amassed $2.25 million total.

> $1.5 million in stocks + $750,000 in bonds =
> $2.25 million
> You sell $500,000 in stocks, leaving $1 million in your
> stock account
> You have $750,000 in bonds + $500,000 transferred
> from stocks into bonds = $1,250,000 in bonds
> $1,250,000 x 6% annual return = $75,000 per year to
> live on in retirement.

Using this method, you should never outlive your money. Every seven years for the rest of your life, you should get an allowance increase. This will also increase your net worth. You can adjust this system to fit your goals and needs. If your health is deteriorating, and you don't have children, you may want to move more money into bonds so you can enjoy additional income immediately. No matter your individual situation, the goal is to have an increasingly better lifestyle while also adding to your assets.

YOUR TO-DO LIST

IT IS A STRAIGHTFORWARD process now. You should have completed the following steps and have the knowledge and confidence to start investing. If you have done your reading, then your research should be a snap. Let's first go over the steps:

1. You have made a priority list and decided that investing is a worthwhile place to spend your time and money. You have decided the life you have now could be better, and you are going to change it for the better. The future you want needs to be planned and not left to chance.

2. You have read Dave Ramsey's *Total Money Makeover* and set up a budget. You have allocated enough money to invest; you spend your money intentionally. You have an emergency fund, thus eliminating the need to sell your stocks in an emergency.

3. You are educating yourself. If you have started from square one, you have read *The Idiot's Guide to Investing*. You have a basic understanding of investing and are ready to move on.

4. You have read *Beating the Street* and *One Up on Wall Street*. You have printed out motivational quotes from Warren Buffett or Peter Lynch to help you gain perspective, which is key.

5. You have read the *Motley Fool Stock Advisor* and subscribe to them or a similar investing service. You understand their investing philosophy and how they analyze a company's financials.

6. You have researched companies and selected a few whose products you love and whose values you understand. Look for these companies via Motley Fool or another service in which you have confidence. Ideally, the Motley Fool recommends them too.

7. Compile your research. Who is the company CEO; how much stock does he own? How long has he been in place? Who are its competitors? Is there a competitive moat? Copy and paste the articles both supporting and opposing your position. Write a synopsis affirming and refuting their claims.

8. Set up a mock portfolio in *Yahoo Finance* with an imaginary sum of $10,000. Divide the amount between your favorite companies (minimum of five, maximum of fifteen).

9. Manage the mock portfolio while you build confidence and knowledge. Update your synopses and company research every quarter.

10. You are ready to start with real money. Create an account and start building your stock portfolio based on the mock portfolio you have monitored. Save and add to these positions when you have the money. If you have fifteen stocks every time you scrape together some spare money, one of them will be on sale.

11. Continue to learn and educate yourself. Grow wealthy and prosper. When the market looks bleak, reread Lynch and Buffet. Realize you will make money when you weather the storm, as people flee in panic.

12. You have developed a long-term plan for your retirement goals.

13. You have an exit strategy.

> *A society grows great when old men plant trees whose shade they know they shall never sit in.*
>
> —Greek Proverb

HAVE AN EXIT PLAN

MR. RAMSEY CALLS THIS changing your family tree, but the concept is the same. Eventually everyone must deal with mortality. It is both an awkward and uncomfortable subject that is impolite to discuss. People seem to think discussing it will somehow hasten the onset of old age and death. I do not believe that to be the case. I have seen people leave estates, large and small, in shambles because they didn't want to deal with it. In case you haven't figured it out yet, you *will* die at some point. I am always amused when people say, "if I die," as if there is a question about it. You *will* die, so make a plan to deal with it. Much like not planning for retirement doesn't make it go away, death doesn't go away either.

If you want things to go as smoothly as possible for your loved ones, you need to prepare a will. If you are concerned about where your amassed fortune will go, you will also need to do some tax preparation. It's imperative that your will executors know your intentions. I alluded earlier to a lot of shenanigans that rich people pull to escape the taxes they purport to support. There are often estate taxes and inheritance taxes. This depends greatly on where you live.

To avoid these types of taxes, many wealthy people create trusts and foundations. This is often done via a pass-through trust or other such trusts. This concept allows them to leave assets to their survivors without paying estate and inheritance taxes. Many of these wealthy people put their assets into trusts or foundations because the trusts actually own the assets. The person and their children can often use the assets and derive all the benefits of ownership without paying the taxes. For instance, the trust may own a car, a Leer jet, or a vacation home that the trustees use at their leisure. The person who sets up the trust maintains control of it, but they may not technically own it anymore.

Personally, I plan to buy a large tract of land and place it in a trust. I then plan to make it a retreat for extended family where we can all hang out, hunt, fish, and spend time together. How often have you witnessed someone who worked hard, saved, and invested their entire lives to provide for their children? As soon as they pass away, their kids sell their life's work for pennies on the dollar. I would very much like to avoid this by teaching my kids the lessons laid out in this book. Ideally, they will be financially secure so they won't need anything I may leave them. I believe if they can't make it on their own, they probably won't be able to hold on to whatever I leave them either.

A large ranch or farm would afford my family the luxury of always having a roof over their heads and a place to spend time for generations after I'm gone. I hope to enjoy it for the remainder of my years on earth, and then leave it for my descendants to enjoy for a while. I think life should be enjoyed responsibly; that takes planning and hard work. I would like to leave my children better off than I am and hopefully they will do the same for each succeeding generation.

I heard somewhere that instead of giving your kids all the things you didn't have, how about teaching them all the things you didn't know? Enjoying your life, blessing your children, and leaving the world a better place are goals I think we should all share. Again, investing and money management is not voodoo magic. It's not easy, nor is it overly complicated. It is primarily based on behavior and knowledge. Improving your life and the lives of your loved ones, or simply obtaining more freedom and security, won't happen unless you *make* it happen. Time will not wait. It won't get easier later, and it's entirely up to you. It will not be okay unless you make it okay.

Instead of giving your kids all the things you didn't have, teach them all the things you didn't know.

Hopefully, you will discover that investing is a worthwhile hobby that greatly enriches your life and the lives of those whom you care about. I have known great poverty, and I have also enjoyed great abundance. I much prefer the latter. Money can be a blessing or a curse. Be the guy with the five talents. Be that good man who leaves an inheritance to his children's children.

Bottom Line: Envision your retirement. Get serious about calculating where you need to be financially to live the lifestyle you desire upon retirement. Health problems and death are unavoidable. Plan to deal with these, and add them to your "Next Steps" list.

ABOUT THE AUTHOR

CHRISTOPHER Q. MCKAY IS just a regular guy who decided he didn't want to die poor. He lives in Roswell, New Mexico with his wife, Lindsey, and their two children. He has over 20 years of experience in personal finance. His quarterly stock research continues to help countless people take charge of their finances and achieve financial success.

GLOSSARY OF TERMS

401k- an arrangement that allows an employee to choose between taking compensation in cash or deferring a percentage of it to an investment account under the plan. The amount deferred is usually not taxable to the employee until it is withdrawn or distributed from the plan. *Investopedia*

Bagger- usually accompanied by a number preceding it. For example, a ten-bagger is an investment that appreciates to 10 times its initial purchase price. The term "tenbagger" was coined by legendary fund manager, Peter Lynch in his book *One Up on Wall Street*. While "tenbagger" can describe any investment that appreciates or has the potential to increase ten-fold, it is usually used to describe stocks with explosive growth prospects. Lynch coined the term because he is an avid baseball fan, and "bag" is a colloquial term for base; thus "tenbagger" represents two home runs and a double, or the stock equivalent of a hugely successful baseball play. *Investopedia*

Bond- a debt investment in which an investor loans money to an entity, (typically corporate or governmental) which borrows the funds for a defined period of time at a variable or fixed interest rate. Bonds are used by companies, municipalities, states and sovereign governments to raise money and finance a variety of projects and activities. Owners of bonds are debt holders, or creditors, of the issuer. *Investopedia*

The Money Talk

Capital Gains tax (CGT)- a type of tax levied on capital gains, profits an investor realizes when he sells a capital asset for a price that is higher than the purchase price. Capital gains taxes are only triggered when an asset is realized, not while it is held by an investor. To illustrate, an investor can own shares that appreciate every year, but the investor does not incur a capital gains tax on the shares until he sells them. *Investopedia*

Certificates of Deposit (CDs)- a savings certificate with a fixed maturity date specified fixed interest rate and can be issued in any denomination aside from minimum investment requirements. A CD restricts access to the funds until the maturity date of the investment. CDs are generally issued by and are insured by the FDIC up to $250,000 per individual. *Investopedia*

Certified public accountant (CPA)- a designation given by the American Institute of Certified Public Accountants to those who pass an exam and meet work experience requirements. *Investopedia*

Compound Interest- Compound interest (or compounding interest) is interest calculated on the initial principal and also on the accumulated interest of previous periods of a deposit or loan. Thought to have originated in 17th-century Italy, compound interest can be thought of as "interest on interest," and will make a sum grow at a faster rate than simple interest, which is calculated only on the principal amount. The rate at which compound interest accrues depends on the frequency of compounding; the higher the number of compounding periods, the greater the compound interest. Thus, the amount of compound interest accrued on $100 compounded at 10% annually will be lower than that on $100 compounded at 5% semi-annually over the same time period. *Investopedia*

Compounding Factor- process where the value of an investment increases because the earnings on an investment, both capital gains and interest, earn interest as time passes. This exponential growth occurs because the total growth of an investment, along with its principal, earn money in the next period. *Investopedia*

Conventional wisdom- the generally accepted belief, opinion, judgment, or prediction about a particular matter. *Merriam-Webster*

Day trading- the act of buying and selling a financial instrument within the same day, or even multiple times over the course of a day, taking advantage of small price moves. Day trading can be a dangerous game for those who are new at it or who don't adhere to a well-thought out method. *Investopedia*

Deflation- a contraction in the supply of circulated money within an economy, and therefore the opposite of inflation. In times of deflation, the purchasing power of currency and wages are higher than they otherwise would have been. *Investopedia*

Dividend- a distribution of a portion of a company's earnings, decided by the board of directors, to a class of its shareholders. Dividends can be issued as cash payments, as shares of stock, or other property. *Investopedia*

Dollar cost average- an investment technique of buying a fixed dollar amount of a particular investment on a regular schedule, regardless of the share price. *Investopedia*

Earned income- income derived from active participation in a trade or business, including wages, salary, tips, commissions and bonuses. This is the opposite of unearned income. *Investopedia*

EBITDA- stands for earnings before interest, taxes, depreciation, and amortization. It is one indicator of a company's financial performance and is used as a proxy for the earning potential of a business, although doing so has its drawbacks. Further, EBITDA strips out the cost of debt capital and its tax effects by adding back interest and taxes to earnings. *Investopedia*

Effective tax rate- the average rate at which an individual or corporation is taxed. The effective tax rate for individuals is the average rate at which their earned income is taxed, and the effective tax rate for a corporation is the average rate at which its pre-tax profits are taxed. An individual's effective tax rate is calculated by dividing total tax expense from line 63 of his 1040 Form by his taxable income from line 43 of that form. *Investopedia*

Emergency fund- money you've saved for those unexpected costs that would otherwise blow your budget—like a midnight trip to the emergency room. *Dave Ramsey*

Forward P/E- a measure of the price-to-earnings (P/E) ratio using forecasted earnings for the P/E calculation. While the earnings used are just an estimate and are not as reliable as current earnings data, there is still benefit in estimated P/E analysis. The forecasted earnings used in the formula can either be for the next 12 months or for the next full-year fiscal period. *Investopedia*

Free market economy- an economy where the law of supply and demand, rather than a central government, regulates production and labor. Companies sell goods and services at the highest price consumers are willing to pay, while workers demand the highest wages companies are willing to pay for their services. A purely capitalist economy is a free market economy; the profit motive drives all commerce and forces businesses to operate as efficiently as possible to avoid losing market share to competitors. *Investopedia*

Front-end load- a commission or sales charge applied at the time of the initial purchase for an investment, usually with mutual funds and insurance policy purchases. It is deducted from the investment amount and, as a result, lowers the size of the investment. Front-end loads are paid to investment intermediaries, such as financial planners, brokers and investment advisors, as sales commissions; as such, these sales charges are not part of a mutual fund's operating expenses. *Investopedia*

Generally Accepted Accounting Principles (GAAP)- a common set of accounting principles, standards and procedures that companies must follow when they compile their financial statements. GAAP is a combination of authoritative standards (set by policy boards) and the commonly accepted ways of recording and reporting accounting information. *Investopedia*

Great Depression- the greatest and longest economic recession of the 20th century and, by some accounts, modern world history. By most contemporary accounts, it began with the U.S. stock market crash of 1929, and didn't completely end until after World War II, in 1946. Economists and historians often cite the Great Depression as the most critical economic event of the 20th century. *Investopedia*

Hedge funds- a fancy name for an investment partnership. It's the marriage of a fund manager, which can often be known as the general partner and the investors in the hedge fund, sometimes known as the limited partners. The limited partners contribute the money and the general partner manages it according to the fund's strategy. A hedge fund's purpose is to maximize investor returns and eliminate risk, hence the word "hedge." *Investopedia*

Inflation- the rate at which the general level of prices for goods and services is rising and, consequently, the purchasing power of currency is falling. Central banks attempt to limit inflation, and avoid deflation in order to keep the economy running smoothly. *Investopedia*

Internal Revenue Service (IRS)- a U.S. government agency responsible for the collection of taxes and enforcement of tax laws. Established in 1862 by President Abraham Lincoln, the agency operates under the authority of the United States Department of the Treasury, and its primary purpose includes the collection of individual income taxes and employment taxes. The IRS also handles corporate, gift, excise and estate taxes. *Investopedia*

Income tax rate- the percentage of an individual's taxable income or a corporation's earnings that is owed to the state, federal and in some cases, municipal governments. The dollar threshold for each tax rate is dependent upon the status of the filer (such as single, married filing separately, married filing jointly and head of household). *Investopedia*

Index mutual fund- a type of mutual fund with a portfolio constructed to match or track the components of a market index, such as the Standard & Poor's 500 Index (S&P 500). An index mutual fund is said to provide broad market exposure, low operating expenses and low portfolio turnover. These funds adhere to specific rules or standards (e.g. efficient tax management or reducing tracking errors) that stay in place no matter the state of the markets. *Investopedia*

Investment- an asset or item that is purchased with the hope that it will generate income or will appreciate in the future. In an economic sense, an investment is the purchase of goods that are not consumed today but are used in the future to create wealth. In finance, an investment is a monetary asset purchased with the idea that the asset will provide income in the future or will be sold at a higher price for a profit. *Investopedia*

Long-term capital gains tax rate- When taxpayers file their returns with the Internal Revenue Service (IRS), they report the net total of their long-term capital gains earned in the tax year. The IRS taxes long-term capital gains at a special capital gains tax rate, which ranges from 0 to 20%, as of 2016, and it depends on the tax filer's income. Investopedia Margin call- an investor receives a margin call from a broker if one or more of the securities he had bought with borrowed money decreases in value past a certain point. The investor must either deposit more money in the account or sell off some of his assets. *Investopedia*

Marginal tax rate- the amount of tax paid on an additional dollar of income. Under a marginal tax rate, tax payers are most often divided into tax brackets or ranges, which determine the rate applied to the taxable income of the tax filer. As income increases, what is earned will be taxed at a higher rate than the first dollar earned. *Investopedia*

Market capitalization- the total dollar market value of a company's outstanding shares. Commonly referred to as "market cap," it is calculated by multiplying a company's shares outstanding by the current market price of one share. *Investopedia*

Market correction- a reverse movement, usually negative, of at least 10% in a stock, bond, commodity or index to adjust for an overvaluation. Corrections are generally temporary price declines interrupting an uptrend in the market or an asset. *Investopedia*

Medicare- a U.S. federal health program that subsidizes people who meet one of the following criteria:
1. An individual aged 65 or older who has been a U.S. citizen or permanent legal resident for five years.
2. An individual who is disabled and has collected Social Security for a minimum of two years.
3. An individual who is undergoing dialysis for kidney failure or who is in need of a kidney transplant.
4. An individual who has Amyotrophic Lateral Sclerosis (Lou Gehrig's disease). Medicare is divided into two parts. The first part of the coverage encompasses in-patient hospital, skilled nursing facility, home health and hospice care. The second part of coverage encompasses almost all the necessary medical services (doctors' services, laboratory and x-ray services, wheelchairs, etc). Investopedia

Mega-cap- The biggest companies in the investment universe, as measured by market capitalization. While there is no exact definition of the term, mega cap generally refers to companies with a market cap exceeding $100 billion. Mega caps are usually household names with strong brand recognition and global operations, such as Exxon Mobil, Apple, Microsoft, Nestle and IBM. *Investopedia*

Micro-cap- A micro-cap is a publicly traded company in the United States that has a market capitalization between approximately $50 million and $300 million. Micro-cap companies have greater market capitalization than nano caps, and less than small-, mid-, large- and mega-cap corporations.

The Money Talk

Companies with larger market capitalization do not automatically have stock prices that are higher than those companies with smaller market capitalizations. *Investopedia*

Mutual fund- an investment vehicle made up of a pool of funds collected from many investors for the purpose of investing in securities such as stocks, bonds, money market instruments and similar assets. Mutual funds are operated by money managers, who invest the fund's capital and attempt to produce capital gains and income for the fund's investors. *Investopedia*

Net worth- Net worth is the amount by which assets exceed liabilities. Net worth is a concept applicable to individuals and businesses as a key measure of how much an entity is worth. A consistent increase in net worth indicates good financial health; conversely, net worth may be depleted by annual operating losses or a substantial decrease in asset values relative to liabilities. *Investopedia*

Penny stocks- typically trade outside of the major market exchanges at a relatively low price and have a small market capitalization. These stocks are generally considered highly speculative and high risk because of their lack of liquidity, large bid-ask spreads, small capitalization and limited following and disclosure. *Investopedia*

(P/E)- ratio of the market price of a company's stock to its earnings per share (EPS). *Investopedia*

Prodigious Accumulators of Wealth (PAW)- reciprocal of the more common UAW, accumulating usually well over the product of the individual's age and one tenth of his/her realized pretax income and are usually considered to be millionaires however, not all are. Thomas Stanley Publicly-traded company- a company that has sold all or a portion of itself to the public via an initial public offering (IPO), meaning shareholders have claim to part of the company's assets and profits. *Investopedia*

152

Roth IRA- an individual retirement plan (a type of qualified retirement plan) that bears many similarities to the traditional IRA. The biggest distinction between the two is how they're taxed. Since traditional IRAs contributions are made with pretax dollars, you pay income tax when you withdraw the money from the account during retirement. Conversely, Roth IRAs are funded with after-tax dollars; the contributions are not tax deductible (although you may be able to take a tax credit of 10 to 50% of the contribution), depending on your income and life situation). But when you start withdrawing funds, these qualified distributions are tax-free. *Investopedia*

Rule of 72- a shortcut to estimate the number of years required to double your money at a given annual rate of return. The rule states that you divide the rate, expressed as a percentage, into 72. *Investopedia*

Short-term capital gain- a capital gain realized by the sale or exchange of a capital asset that has been held for exactly one year or less. Short-term gains are taxed at the taxpayer's top marginal tax rate. *Investopedia*

Simplified Employee Pension Plan (SEP)- a retirement plan established by employers, including self-employed individuals (sole proprietorships or partnerships). The SEP is an IRA-based plan to which employers may make tax-deductible contributions on behalf of eligible employees, including the business owner. The employer is allowed a tax deduction for plan contributions, which are made to each eligible employee's SEP IRA on a discretionary basis. *Investopedia*

Start-up- a company that is in the first stage of its operations. These companies are often initially bankrolled by their entrepreneurial founders as they attempt to capitalize on developing a product or service for which they believe there is a demand. *Investopedia*

Stock certificate- a physical piece of paper representing ownership in a company. Stock certificates will include information such as the number of shares owned, the date, an identification number, usually a corporate seal, and signatures. They are a bit bigger than normal piece of paper and most of them have intricate designs to discourage fraudulent replication. *Investopedia*

Supplemental Security Income (SSI)- a federal program that provides additional income for older and disabled people with little to no income stream. This program helps the participants meet their basic needs by providing them with monthly cash distributions. The program is funded by tax revenues received by the government. *Investopedia*

Tax avoidance- the use of legal methods to modify an individual's financial situation to lower the amount of income tax owed. *Investopedia*

Tax evasion- a willful and especially criminal attempt to evade the imposition or payment of a tax. *Merriam-Webster*

Term-life insurance- A type of life insurance with a limited coverage period. Once that period or "term" is up, it is up to the policy owner to decide whether to renew or to let the coverage end. This type of insurance policy contrasts with permanent life insurance, which is intended to provide life-long protection. Other characteristics of term insurance include:

Low cost, no cash value, usually renewable, and sometimes convertible to permanent life insurance. *Investopedia*

Treasury bill (T-bill)- a short-term debt obligation backed by the U.S. government with a maturity of less than one year, sold in denominations of $1,000 up to a maximum purchase of $5 million. T-bills have various maturities and are issued at a discount from par. When an investor purchases a T-Bill, the U.S. government writes an IOU. Investors do not receive regular payments as with a coupon bond, but a T-Bill pays an interest rate. *Investopedia*

Traditional IRA- allows individuals to direct pretax income towards investments that can grow tax-deferred; no capital gains or dividend income is taxed until it is withdrawn. Individual taxpayers are allowed to contribute 100% of any earned compensation up to a specified maximum dollar amount. Contributions to a traditional IRA may be tax-deductible depending on the taxpayer's income, tax-filing status and other factors. *Investopedia*

Trailing P/E- calculated by taking the current stock price and dividing it by the trailing earnings per share (EPS) for the past 12 months. This measure differs from forward P/E, which uses earnings estimates for the next four quarters. As a result, forward P/E can sometimes be more relevant to investors when evaluating a company. *Investopedia*

Under Accumulators of Wealth (UAW)- used to represent individuals who have a low net wealth compared to their income. A $250,000 per year doctor is an "Under Accumulator of Wealth" if his/her net worth is less than the product of their age and one tenth of his/her realized pretax income. *Thomas Stanley*

Unearned income- describes any personal income that comes from investments and other sources unrelated to employment services. Examples of unearned income include interest from a savings account, bond interest, alimony and dividends from stock. This type of income differs from traditionally earned income, which is the income earned from active work or business activity. *Investopedia*

Whole-life insurance- a policy that provides lifetime protection by paying a lump sum death benefit. Whole life policies differ from term insurance in that they have a savings component with earning accruing referred to as cash value. With this type of insurance, a policy holder may take loans against the cash value which usually have a minimum guaranteed rate of interest. *Investopedia*

ENDNOTES

[1] Dave Ramsey, *The Total Money Makeover: A Proven Plan for Financial Fitness* (Thomas Nelson, 2003).

[2] Sir Isaac Newton, *The Correspondence of Isaac Newton* (Cambridge University Press, 1975).

[3] Holy Bible, New International Version®, NIV®, Biblica, Inc.,1973, 1978, 1984, 2011).

[4] Mary Baker Eddy, "Liberty and Government," *The Christian Science Journal* (1902), 465.

[5] Avery Scoville, message to author, January, 2016.

[6] Robert Kyosaki and Sharon Lechter, *Rich Dad Poor Dad* (Warner Books ed., 2000).

[7] Matt. 19:24 NIV.

[8] Thomas J. Stanley and William D. Danko, *The Millionaire Next Door*, (New York: Pocket Books, 1996).

[9] Thomas Sowell, *Wealth, Poverty, and Politics* (Basic Books, 2015).

[10] "Like Lottery Winners, Pro Athletes Also Blow Big Money," The Huffington Post blog, accessed June 21, 2017, http://www.huffingtonpost.com/don-mcnay/like-lottery-winners-pro_b_294275.html.

[11] Dave Ramsey, Dave Ramsey Radio Show, http://www.daveramsey.com/show.

[12] Define conventional wisdom, Merriam-Webster, accessed June 21, 2017, https://www.merriam-webster.com/dictionary/conventional%20wisdom.

[13] Shawn Achor, *The Happiness Advantage* (Crown Business, 2010).

Endnotes

[14] *The Reader's Digest*, September 1947, 64.

[15] Thomas Sowell, *Wealth, Poverty, and Politics* (Basic Books, 2015).

[16] Dave Ramsey, *The Total Money Makeover: A Proven Plan for Financial Fitness* (Thomas Nelson, 2003).

[17] "The Dunning-Kruger Effect Shows Why Some People Think They're Great Even When Their Work is Terrible," accessed June 21, 2017, https://www.forbes.com/sites/markmurphy/2017/01/24/the-dunning-kruger-effect-shows-why-some-people-think-theyre-great-even-when-their-work-is-terrible/#c7f8f785d7c9.

[18] Dave Ramsey, *The Total Money Makeover: A Proven Plan for Financial Fitness* (Thomas Nelson, 2003).

[19] Jeff Rose, "Average Retirement Savings by Age – How Does Your Savings Stack Up?" Good Financial Cents, June 7, 2012.

[20] Nanci Hellmich, "One-Third Have Almost No Retirement Savings," *USA Today*, April 22, 2015.

[21] *Wizard of Oz*. Film. Directed by Victor Fleming. Metro-Goldwyn-Mayer (MGM), 1939.

[22] Dave Ramsey, *The Total Money Makeover: A Proven Plan for Financial Fitness* (Thomas Nelson, 2003).

[23] "Zig Ziglar Quotes," Good Reads, accessed June 22, 2017, http://www.goodreads.com/quotes/78121-if-you-aim-at-nothing-you-will-hit-it-every.

[24] Demi, *One Grain of Rice: A Mathematical Folktale* (New York: Scholastic Press, 1997).

[25] Adam Mayers, "How Warren Buffett made 94 percent of his wealth after he turned 60," *The Star*, December 11, 2014, https://www.thestar.com/business/personal_finance/spending_saving/2014/12/11/start_saving_young_and_watch_small_amounts_grow_mayers.html.

[26] *A Taxing Trend: The Rise in Complexity, Forms, and Paperwork Burdens by David* (Keating, April 15, 2009).

[27] *Money Magazine*.

[28] Dave Ramsey, *The Total Money Makeover: A Proven Plan for Financial Fitness* (Thomas Nelson, 2003).

[29] Peter Lynch, *One Up on Wall Street* (Simon & Schuster, second edition, 2000).
[30] Jeremy Hsu, "The Truth About Skydiving Risks," *Live Science*, March 26, 2009, https://www.livescience.com/5350-truth-skydiving-risks.html.
[31] Gregory Wallace, "Odds of winning the Powerball jackpot: One in 175,000,000," CNN, February 11, 2015, http://money.cnn.com/2015/02/09/pf/powerball-jackpot-odds/index.html.
[32] Benjamin Graham, *The Intelligent Advisor* (New York: HarperCollins Publishers, Inc., 1973).

92333854R00095

Made in the USA
San Bernardino, CA
31 October 2018